# NO-
# REGRET
# DECISIONS

# NO-REGRET DECISIONS

## Making Good Choices
## During Difficult Times

# Shannon Lee Simmons

**Collins**

Published by Collins, an imprint of HarperCollins Publishers Ltd

First edition

HarperCollins books may be purchased for educational, business or
sales promotional use through our Special Markets Department.

HarperCollins Publishers Ltd
Bay Adelaide Centre, East Tower
22 Adelaide Street West, 41st Floor
Toronto, Ontario, Canada
M5H 4E3

*www.harpercollins.ca*

Library and Archives Canada Cataloguing in Publication

Title: No-regret decisions : making good choices during difficult times /
Shannon Lee Simmons.
Names: Simmons, Shannon Lee, author.
Identifiers: Canadiana (print) 20220390592 | Canadiana (ebook) 20220390630 |
ISBN 9781443463454 (softcover) | ISBN 9781443463461 (EPUB)
Subjects: LCSH: Decision making. | LCSH: Life change events.
Classification: LCC BF448 .S538 2023 | DDC 153.8/3—dc23

Printed and bound in the United States of America

LSC/C 9 8 7 6 5 4 3 2 1

*For Matt, Billy, and Teddy.*
*I love you so much!*

# CONTENTS

# NOTE FROM THE AUTHOR

The stories in this book are real. The people are my clients, each of whom had to make life-altering decisions during a difficult time in their life: divorce, retirement, or midlife crisis, while becoming a caregiver, or while dealing with fertility or job loss.

The conversations had and the emotions expressed are real—I didn't sugar-coat them. Each person in this book has given me express permission to tell their story, although their names and any identifying factors have been changed for privacy.

It's also important to note that all advice given in this book assumes that a person's basic needs for food, shelter, and personal freedoms are being met and that their personal safety is intact.

# INTRODUCTION

If you're reading this book, you probably need to make some really difficult decisions during a really difficult time. You've found yourself in what I call a "decision crisis" and are likely experiencing a ton of uncertainty about the future. Unfortunately, there is no turning back. The emotional and financial stakes are high, but you have to make big decisions whether you like it or not.

You're facing a lot. So take a deep breath. You're in the right place. I can help.

I'm a certified financial planner, life coach, and collaborative divorce professional who has been on the front lines of financial planning and life coaching for over 15 years. My job is to help people navigate complex decisions during major transitions in their lives. Divorce, critical illness, buying your first house, becoming a caregiver, family planning, infertility, death of loved ones, job losses, retirement ... You know, life.

I often joke that my job is 90% life coaching and 10% financial spreadsheets, which is what I love most about my work and this book. My previous two books were financial planning advice with a side of coaching. This one is different. It's a life-coaching book with a side of financial planning: 90% life coaching and 10% spreadsheet.

This book is for people whose lives have been, or are about to be, turned upside down, forcing them into a situation where they need, or want, to make big, potentially life-altering decisions. Decisions with high emotional and financial stakes, made without knowing what their *next normal* will look like—what their daily life will be *after* making these huge upcoming decisions.

This book will teach you how to make difficult decisions today, tomorrow, and 10 years from now. Decisions you can look back on and say, "I wouldn't have done it any other way," no matter how things ended up playing out.

I call these "no-regret decisions"—the kinds of decisions that give you hope for the future and restore your confidence in your ability to handle anything that life throws your way.

If you're experiencing a major life transition, uncertainty about your future can be terrifying, and you're likely in panic mode a lot of the time. If there's one thing I know after helping people navigate complex choices, it's that your outlook today will dictate the decisions you make and that those decisions can impact the next version of your daily life. You are creating your next normal, one decision at a time.

That may feel like a lot of pressure, but it's also awesome! Even though you may be having a rough time right now and don't want to make the decisions that lie in front of you, it's comforting to know that maybe, just maybe, you have a smidgen of control over the outcome. To me, that's a relief.

I've been through my own personal crises and major life transitions, too. I moved out West for love and realized the moment my plane landed that I was so wrong and should have *never* come. I was heartbroken, living on the other side of the country without friends or family, and I had to decide if I should stay or go home. *Oof.*

Then came the time when I wanted to quit my high-rollin' Bay Street job to start my own business but was scared to leave the golden handcuffs behind. I had to decide whether to quit or stay. I decided to follow my dream, but it didn't work out right away and I couldn't afford my new life. Defeated, I had to empty out my savings, take on credit card debt, and then decide if I should keep going or give up. *Eek!*

Most recently, I faced the challenge of parenting my children while juggling work-from-home during the COVID-19 pandemic and ensuing lockdowns that turned the world upside down starting in March 2020. *Ugh.*

During the first weeks of lockdown, I was exhausted and frazzled. Faced with the unknown, my adrenalin levels skyrocketed on a daily basis. Both my husband and I were fortunate to have full-time jobs that allowed us to work from home, but with childcare having been abruptly closed, we were also trying to take care of a 6-month-old baby and a 2 ½-year-old toddler. Every day was a sprint. Total chaos.

I knew I was lucky: We were all healthy. My husband, Matt, and I didn't work on the front lines. I had nothing to complain about and so much to be grateful for. But I still felt scared and frenzied and guilty all the time.

I had over 200 (remote) meetings during the first lockdown. It was tax season, so my schedule was packed with back-to-back tax meetings and emergency financial planning sessions. I was painfully aware of how many of my clients had been laid off and were struggling to secure financial support. They were all counting on me to be there for them, to help them navigate everything financial. On top of that, I felt the weight of being there for my team at work while also being a strong emotional support for my kids. Most days I barely made it through a client session, team call, or media interview without bursting into tears as soon as I hung up.

Sometimes, I didn't make it.

The day the Canadian Emergency Response Benefit (CERB) was announced, I locked myself in our bathroom so I could do an interview (my seventh of the day) in the shower stall, where I'd hoped the interviewer couldn't hear my crying toddler on the other side of the door.

She could hear him. She asked me if I was okay. (*What is it about that question?*) I shut my eyes tightly and, even though I knew she couldn't see me, shook my head without saying a word. I couldn't answer without crying. We stayed on the phone, silently, listening to the sound of my toddler wailing for me while Matt tried to calm him down. Then she broke the silence with a simple "I know. It's impossible."

Later on, at the end of that particularly tough workday, I went into the kitchen to make dinner. The radio was playing in the background and, in what seemed to be a cruel twist of fate, I could hear a parenting expert being interviewed. The host of the show asked, "So how do we parent positively during a pandemic?"

The guest didn't miss a beat, responding that this was our new normal and that we all just needed to focus on the good things we still had in our lives. According to the expert, appreciation was the antidote to fear.

I remember glaring at the radio and shouting in my head, *Stop talking! This isn't normal and none of this is okay!*

My husband's workday ended, and I heard him dashing up the basement stairs to help with the kids and dinner, as always. Matt came into the kitchen to find me crying over a pot of macaroni, trying to hide the tears from my kids.

"What's wrong?"

"Nothing," I blubbered. "Everything."

"I know," he said.

"What if we can't beat it?" I asked, my eyes wide and full of tears. "What if this is it? What if things never go back to normal?"

I was in crisis and trying so hard not to be.

He hugged me tightly. "It will. This isn't forever. It's going to be okay."

"Mommy?" my toddler said softly from the kitchen door. I quickly wiped my eyes before turning around with a big smile.

"What's up, baby?" I asked.

"Are you happy?" he asked.

My tears threatened all over again.

"Of course," I lied, wiping snot from my face before getting down on my knees to his level. I looked him right in the eyes and took hold of his hands. "Of course Mommy is happy."

"Is it the virus?"

He knew. He was not yet 3, but he knew.

In those first few days of the inaugural lockdown, if my toddler caught me crying, I'd lie and say I had a boo-boo or a tummy ache. How could I explain a global pandemic without scaring him? But, 3 weeks in, he had witnessed too many hushed and intense conversations and learned words like "virus" and "lockdown." He was sad that his daycare was closed, the parks were closed, his soccer was closed. He missed Nana and Papa and hated virtual calls and hated me doing virtual work calls even more. It broke my heart.

I focused on my son's face and thought about my next response. What was the best choice? Keep pretending nothing was wrong when nothing was right? Nope.

I was stressed and terrified, but in that moment I knew I needed to change my outlook if I wanted to make good decisions for myself and my family. And that started with honesty.

"Yes," I said at last and then hugged him. "It is the virus."

"I really miss school," he said gloomily.

I kissed his head. "Me too, baby. Me too."

"When will things be okay again?" he asked, his big eyes looking right into mine.

"I don't know," I said. Then I smiled. "But you know what? It's not forever. It's just for now."

"Promise?" he asked.

I steadied myself. "I promise."

I gave him a big squeeze and another kiss and hoped I hadn't just lied to him. Then he ran off to watch TV. Again.

"You okay?" Matt asked.

I nodded. "Ya, I'm good. Just a low moment. I'm fine."

"Sure?" he asked again.

"Sure."

He didn't look convinced but left to get the boys ready for dinner.

"It's just for now," I said aloud to myself, like a mantra, while I put mac-and-cheese on a plate and smashed up some veggies for the baby. *For now*," I repeated resolutely and headed out to the table.

I always thought I was good in a crisis, but everything I knew about myself and my life changed overnight with the onset of the pandemic. The uncertainty around when or if it would be over, combined with grief for my former life, fear for my family's well-being, and anxiety over the state of the world, kept me mired in panic mode for months—soul-crushing, 24/7, could-cry-at-any-moment panic mode.

This acute panic was a problem. I needed to be clear-headed. As the pandemic wore on, I had to start making big decisions. Decisions with high emotional and financial stakes and uncertain outcomes. Do I put my oldest back in preschool when/if it ever opens? Will I have to quit my business for the next few years if I don't have consistent childcare? Should I bail on writing this book?

Every day brought new decisions. And big or small—it didn't matter—every choice was fraught and terrifying. I worried because I knew that the big decisions I made now would dictate how my life would play out for me on a daily basis on the other side of the pandemic (my next normal), whenever that would be.

That first COVID-19 lockdown and the personal crisis that followed caused a shift in myself I never anticipated. An eternal optimist with a can-do attitude, I've always been an overachiever, all of the time. It's part of my identity. (I'm a Capricorn . . . so is Dolly Parton.) But being in panic mode 24/7 made me want to throw in the towel on so many of my dreams, including writing this book.

In fact, the reason I was crying over the macaroni that day was because I had just written my agent telling her I needed to bail on this book.

> *Hey Martha,*
> *I can't write the book without childcare.*
> *I can't write the book when life is this scary and chaotic. I don't think this is ending any time soon and I just can't do it. I'm so sorry.*

It took a pandemic to finally slow me down.

Panic had turned me into a person I didn't recognize. It made me want to hide from my life. Move from a city that I love to somewhere else with a backyard and a lawn. "Well, if the parks are closed now, they will probably close every time there are new cases," I said to my husband before bed one night. "We need a backyard so the kids have somewhere to be outside. We need to move."

The situation left me unmotivated to do anything with my business beyond keeping the lights on because my brain was so overwhelmed. This, of course, led to guilt about letting down the eight people who counted on me to lead our company through this unprecedented situation, which led to more sleepless nights. Round and round it went. Panic, guilt, panic, guilt, and not a lot of sleep.

As the pandemic wore on, I remained in panic mode even though my peers, pals, and colleagues seemed to be adjusting. Unlike them, I still felt shocked and surprised every day. One mention of increased cases on the radio could send me into a dizzying tailspin of fret and despair.

I think it's natural to be in panic mode when your life gets turned upside down by a global pandemic. There's nothing wrong with that. Dare I say it's normal? But I was stuck inside it, unable to see a way out.

The problem with being stuck comes when you start to make big life decisions while *in* panic mode. Panic mode is the *definition* of scarcity mindset, and there's nothing growth-oriented about scarcity mindset. I'll explain more about that later in the book.

It took me some time to realize that my daily panic was not only not helping anything but was making everything worse, robbing me of hope and faith that things would eventually get better. Trying to bail on this book, to move away, to quit my business were all short-term, self-defence strategies meant to make me feel less scared in the moment. The logic was that if I lowered the emotional and financial stakes of my current daily life—no book, no business, no waiting for parks to be open again—I could breathe, feel relief, and not worry so much. But panic lies. The worry would still be there, the juggling would still be there, it would just look different, and it would come with a whole lot of guilt, dissatisfaction, and an investment in a lawn mower.

The pandemic was unexpected and everything about it was beyond my control, forcing me to live my daily life in a totally different way. A way that made me sad and scared. The outcome was entirely uncertain, which made every new daily decision stressful. Worse still, panic kept urging me to make black-and-white, fear-based decisions. (More on fear-based decisions later too.)

I know now that if I had turned my back on this book, if I had moved out of the city and closed my business, I would have created a terrible future for myself. Those choices would have been short-term bandages but long-term mistakes, landing me in a life I wouldn't want for myself later on, after the crisis of the pandemic had passed. The short-term relief that quitting my life would have given me did not outweigh the major long-term benefits of seeing it through, yet I waffled every single day.

I think about that day I told my agent I simply could not write this book and then cried in the kitchen. And then I remember that after dinner that same night, we made a big fort in the living room. Then we went upstairs for bath time and bedtime stories, and I sang both boys to sleep. It was wonderful and predictable. It was utterly and completely normal.

After bedtime, something clicked for me. I went downstairs with a smile on my face. I opened up my email and responded to my agent to ignore my previous email. I could, in fact, write this book. I wasn't going to bail on it. I was going to try because, in that moment, I knew it was the right decision for Future Shannon, even though Current Shannon was not a happy camper.

It occurred to me that I was able to get that kind of logical clarity because I was feeling hopeful in that moment. Hope that came from the fact that I felt, well, *normal.* I felt safe and happy. Even in the chaos of a global pandemic, our dinner, bath, bed, and beyond ritual was still the same. These routines brought me such comfort at a time when pretty much all my of my daily habits had been disrupted. The rituals made me feel safe, happy, and therefore, hopeful, even if just for the evening. These positive feelings put panic mode on pause, momentarily restoring my faith that this chaos wasn't forever; it was just for now. I guess you could say I wasn't afraid because I was appreciating the silver linings in my life . . . just like that happy-go-lucky parenting expert had talked about. *Damn.*

Breaking the cycle of panic allowed me to be present, to clear my head and make good long-term decisions for myself and my family. Decisions that I knew I would not regret later because they would represent what is *truly* important to me. All I wanted at the end of the day was to be able to look back at the choices I made while I was in crisis and say, "I made the best decisions I could, given the circumstances."

For me, that meant writing the book, staying in our current home, and figuring out a solution to keep growing my business, regardless of lockdowns, inconsistent childcare, or closed parks.

And there it is. The key to making decisions that you can be proud of later. Decisions that will make you say, "I wouldn't have done anything differently," regardless of the outcome. Those all-important *no-regret decisions* are the key to trusting yourself to make good choices even when the financial and emotional stakes are high and the future is uncertain.

I'd been coaching my clients with this recipe for no-regret decisions for years, whether they were getting divorced, becoming a caregiver, going through a breakup or job loss— whatever life had thrown at them.

In that wonderful hope-filled moment, I realized that I just needed to practise what I had been preaching.

# CHAPTER 1:

## The Decision Crisis Playbook

So how do you make no-regret decisions when you are in crisis? You follow the guidelines in what I call the *Decision Crisis Playbook*.

### THE DECISION CRISIS PLAYBOOK

1. Don't make decisions in panic mode. Find a hopeful outlook, even if just for a moment.
2. Make long-term, values-based decisions versus short-term, relief-seeking decisions.
3. Control what you can, if you can.

4. Set boundaries, or guardrails, so you don't run out of time or money.
5. Embrace your next normal.

When you find yourself in a decision crisis, be it life-altering or momentary, you can use the Decision Crisis Playbook to make no-regret decisions. The Playbook works, it's repeatable, and it will ensure you not only survive your decision crisis but thrive later, regardless of the outcome.

## WHAT IS A DECISION CRISIS?

Difficult decisions in difficult times. When life as you knew it vanishes and your next normal awaits (often without your permission). A *decision crisis* is very much character-ized by the uncertainty about future outcomes combined with the need to make major decisions at the worst possi-ble time.

Just lost your job? Should you take the lesser-paying job right away or wait it out and hope for a different job with a more livable wage? Recently separated? Do you buy out your ex-partner's share of the matrimonial home or take your half of the sale of the house and move on? I've spent the last 15-plus years helping people navigate all manner of decision crises. Major. Life. Decisions.

Over the years, I've come to identify a decision crisis sit-uation as follows:

Uncertain outcome (loss of power) + High stakes
(emotional or financial) + Difficult decision(s)

The most stressful part of a decision crisis are the choices, or series of choices, you need to make while stressed out: You're in a situation that feels bad and scary. Now, add the need to make critical decisions that will have a huge impact on your life, not only in the short run but also the long run. *No pressure!*

I'm not talking about simple decisions like should you order takeout tonight or not. I'm talking about massive, life-altering decisions. Do you move to England to follow a dream but leave behind your family in Canada? Do you divorce your partner who you respect but don't love anymore? Do you freeze your eggs to give yourself the option to have kids later? These are complicated questions with complex constraints and multiple outcomes with no certainty of how any decision will play out. Each mega decision comes with numerous micro decisions and high emotional and financial stakes. It *is* scary. You don't want to make the wrong choice and have regret. Regret robs you of confidence and peace of mind. And that's what this whole book is really about: finding your way out of a crisis and back to a place of confidence and peace of mind.

At some point in life, we all have to navigate a personal crisis. Some small, some life-altering. There are two types of decision crises that I work through with my clients on a weekly basis: *external decision crises* and *crossroads decision crises*.

An external decision crisis is thrust upon us: a colicky newborn, a death in the family, a messy breakup, a bad traffic accident, a job loss, a pandemic.

A crossroads decision crisis, however, is the result of locking ourselves into behaviours and choices that violate our own core values. In a crossroads decision crisis, things sneak up on us, over time. Think midlife crisis or career crisis. Nothing happened to you, per se, but you kind of wake up one day and realize, "This can't be my life anymore." Living a life that violates your core values day after day will only lead to stress, anxiety, and guilt.

In both kinds of decision crises, the future is uncertain, the emotional and financial stakes are high, and you have to make decisions to see your way through. There is no way to avert it. You're already in it.

The Decision Crisis Playbook is your survival guide, not only mapping out the decision-making process so you have one less thing to worry about while you're going through it, but also ensuring that you'll trust your decision-making process now, next year, and 10 years from now.

The cool thing about my job is that I meet with people year after year. I see them before, during, and after a crisis, so I get to see how their decisions played out. I see who thrived and who did not. The difference always comes back to the same thing: Those who thrived *after* a decision crisis made no-regret decisions.

## THE THREE PHASES OF EVERY DECISION CRISIS

There are three distinct phases in every decision crisis:

1. Panic mode (when hope is gone).
2. The messy middle (when you have to make decisions and are completely over it).
3. Your next normal (when the dust settles and it is what it is).

Let's break down each of these so you can figure out exactly where you are, right now, in your decision crisis.

### Phase 1: Panic Mode

If you're in panic mode right now, it means you're afraid of what comes next. The one common denominator of panic mode is fear. A primal, primitive, hard-wired fear that there isn't enough and there won't be enough. A scarcity mindset.

Research shows that our reptilian brain—the oldest, most underdeveloped part—houses that fear. Scarcity mindset was necessary for survival back when we needed to follow our food sources, which were always moving. But when our 21st-century lives get turned upside down, that kind of pre-historic panic is dangerous. When we're in panic mode, fear flows into every part of our physical bodies, making our hearts race and our mouths go dry.

Scarcity mindset keeps us in fight or flight mode, which forces us to make trade-offs and engage in black-and-white thinking: if this, then that, with no room for options or

nuance. This is detrimental to your decision-making process, which is detrimental to living with no regrets when it
is all over.

Here are some examples of black-and-white thinking:

- I'm in debt, therefore I'm going to be broke
  forever.
- I'm getting divorced; therefore I'm going to die
  alone.
- My preschooler is in lockdown; therefore he's
  never going to learn how to socialize.

Panic mode is stressful and exhausting. The constant
worry and anxiety keeps us up at night. We begin to over-
value immediate, short-term benefits just to give ourselves
a break or a flash of joy in the moment. Relief. That relief,
though, can often come at the expense of future benefits
that would make much more logical sense in the long run.
But in panic mode, we can't think about the long term, just
as we can't see an end to what is happening to us. The timing
couldn't be worse to make big decisions in your life.

Decision crises come in many sizes, from short term to
years on end. Here's an example of a short-term decision crisis: You're on your way to your best friend's wedding. You're
on a layover, waiting for your flight. You're in the wedding
party. Even worse, it's a small wedding and you're one of the
four people standing up for the happy couple. It's Friday.
The wedding is Saturday at noon. You're expected to arrive
tonight so you can be there for the rehearsal dinner Friday

evening. Then, an unexpected blizzard blows in. Flights are being cancelled up and down the departures board. You're worried your flight will be cancelled too. You wait, nervously. Then suddenly, all flights for the night are cancelled. *Shit.*

You immediately begin to panic, ramping up your heartbeat, pulling the knots in your stomach tighter, making you regret the fact that you're just sitting there, doing nothing. You're stuck at the airport. The lineup to talk to a customer service rep is hours long. You can't get through on the airline customer service toll-free phone number.

You have no control, certainly not over the weather or when flights will resume. You already know you're going to miss the rehearsal dinner. *Double shit.*

In a short-term decision crisis situation, there's a ton of uncertainty and the emotional and financial stakes are high: You could take a chance on a later flight, but there's no guarantee that one won't also be cancelled. On top of which, booking now will cost three times the price of your original ticket, and you can't afford to add thousands of dollars to your credit card. But you don't want to miss the wedding either.

Panic wants to shove you into trade-off thinking. Overspend your way out of the situation or miss the wedding completely? Those appear to be your only choices. Panic wants you to believe that you need to decide now, *right now*. But is that true? Certainly, those are two options, but maybe there are more? The point is, while you're in panic mode, you can't tell the difference between logic, gut instinct, and a terrible idea. You need to give yourself time to evaluate your options more clearly.

You can't access your logical brain if you're constantly distracted by thoughts that tell you you're not good enough or that there isn't enough time, money, or choices. The only way to turn off the fear and panic is to strive to feel safe and happy *at the same time*. You can't have one without the other. Safe without happy is not enough. Happy without safe is also not enough. It's the act of striving toward the balance between *both* that is key. Also, it's important to understand that you don't "move through" a crisis in a linear way; you don't graduate out of panic and into hope for good. You have to constantly find your way back to hope along the way. It takes effort and consistency.

## Safe + Happy = Hope

This is the key to getting out of panic mode. Hope lifts you out of your fear and into a place where you can see above the moment and through the panic. A place where you become open to options, can choose clearly, and can stop black-and-white trade-off thinking so you don't make decisions based on short-term wins at long-term costs. Remember: You don't want to regret your choices on the other side of the crisis.

There is a school of thought out there that believes hope and optimism can be damaging in times of crisis. I read about this in a personal essay by Admiral James Stockdale, who was a prisoner of war in Vietnam for 7 years. Stockdale claimed that optimism is similar to anxiety in that it provides a distorted view that pretends to be self-protective but is not. He explained that optimism comes from wishful thinking and that wishful thinking can lead to massive disappointment, which is even worse for our hearts. When he was a prisoner of war, Stockdale said that the optimists died first in the prison. They told themselves they'd be out by Christmas, and when the holiday rolled around again and they were still in prison, they died of broken hearts. Stockdale believed that the optimists died of exhaustion because their brains kept casting backward and forward, imagining solutions to end their present horrors that did not corroborate with reality. While he said you must never lose faith that you'll prevail in the end, he recommended realism and endurance to confront the brutal facts of your current situation instead of wishful thinking.

Now, here I am, touting a hopeful outlook if only to give you a short reprieve from panic. But I've thought about this a lot and I stand by my hopeful outlook for a decision crisis. I agree with the admiral that endurance is the name of the game if your basic safety, personal freedoms, water, food, and shelter needs are being threatened with no end in sight. But these are not the types of decision crises we are talking about in this book. In this book, a decision crisis means you have to make big decisions at a really difficult time but your basic needs for food and shelter are met, and your personal freedoms and security are intact. That's the difference. That's why moments of hope are absolutely critical. Hope allows you to create options and not get stuck in the trade-off thinking of scarcity mindset.

I'm not saying you have to be a Pollyanna optimist. If you're a natural pessimist, that's okay. Maybe even better.

You'll add a side of realism to the optimism pie that could be *chef's kiss* perfect for you.

The point of hope is not to pretend that your bad time isn't happening. It's not to wash over the pain you're feeling with a toxic "everything's gonna be okay" mantra. And it's certainly not to set you up for severe disappointment. Quite the opposite. When trying to get yourself out of panic mode, striving to feel safe and happy at the same time is meant to give you a hopeful outlook, if only momentarily–long enough that you can see, create, and gather meaningful options for yourself, which will allow you to make a decision you won't regret.

Over the years, I've found that the most effective ways people pull themselves out of panic mode is to recreate a life that feels 60% normal, to create micro timelines and micro goals, and to ensure there is a circle of care.

When there's too much change all at once, it can catapult most of us into panic mode. Doing what you can to feel normal can help you to catch your breath while leaving some mental bandwidth free for the new changes. When dealing with uncertainty, it's hard to know how to make plans 3 days from now. You can regain control by using micro timelines and setting micro goals. Lastly, you need to not feel isolated in your panic. You need to create a circle of care for yourself with people who understand you and know what you're dealing with. These are the tools that will help you pop out of panic mode so you can clearly see the forest for the trees.

Once you pull yourself out of panic mode you can start to look at the difficult decisions you must make. This happens during the messy middle phase of your Decision Crisis Playbook. The messy middle is the time when your shock has subsided. You're exhausted. And while you're over the initial panic, you're still surrounded by uncertainty and need to move forward. You can't put off making decisions any longer.

The messy middle is when you have to play your hand.

### Phase 2: The Messy Middle

A decision crisis is like a poker hand. You get the cards you're dealt, whether you like it or not. The outcome is entirely unpredictable, there's only so much good information you can confirm (your own cards are all you have), and you have to decide how best to play them. Do you up the ante? Do you hold? Do you fold? Can you really read the person across the table? Can you actually control or predict anything in the situation?

For most people, decisions start with a quick cost-benefit analysis: What's at stake? Is it more than money? Is it your reputation? If you lose (a.k.a. choose "wrong"), will the game (your next normal) still be fun? Once you know what matters most to you in that round of poker, you'll assess the benefit of honouring those values against the risk (the cost) and make a choice. You'll play your hand and see what happens.

When the cards are revealed, you'll see where the chips fall. If luck is on your side, great. If not, you can't blame yourself. You will have made the best decision you could with the information available. You could not control the outcome, and fretting about it once it's happened is the same as fretting over the rain. It is, as they say, what it is. There is no way you can change a thing.

In life, decision-making is much more complex than a card game. There are so many outcomes, and the stakes are your deeper personal values mixed with time and financial constraints. But the idea is the same: You can only predict so much.

Unlike a poker game, where decisions have to be made quickly, crisis situations often have longer decision-making timelines. The longer you have to make a decision, the messier and more unpredictable things get. And the messier the middle becomes. You need to ensure you're making decisions that uphold your core values, provide you with some short-term control (where possible), and don't leave you with regret because you ran out of time or money.

Let's look at our wedding crisis example again. If you're that person at the airport, you need to allow yourself enough time to gather all the information needed to create options:

- How much will it actually cost to book on another airline?
- What is the weather forecast?
- How much is a rental car and would you make it in time if you drove?
- Would you be happy if you missed the wedding?

There is so much information to gather, and it's important to look at both the good and the bad. What is in your control and what is not? Once you've gathered all the information and mapped out your best- and worst-case scenarios, you'll be able to choose the best outcome for yourself. You might even find a solution somewhere in the middle of best and worst.

Is your worst-case scenario missing the wedding? Or is your worst-case scenario spending three times the ticket price and having debt for months?

It comes down to understanding what matters most to *you*. Which core value is more crucial at this particular time in your life? Is it coming through for your best friend or avoiding months spent paying down that extra ticket after you just became debt free? Both are totally valid options, but you need to think about what's best for *you*.

Understanding what is truly most important to you, not what you think *should* be important, will lead to decisions based on something I call your "deciding value(s)" and, therefore, long-term happiness on the other side of the decision crisis. If your worst-case scenario is missing the wedding, then you know you are going at any cost. The rest is just details, namely finding a way to make it happen for the lowest price.

When comparing the drive versus fly options, driving looks cheaper but comes also comes with risk. What if the roads are bad due to the storm? It's a long way. You'd have to drive 20 hours straight and then basically go directly to the wedding from the car–if you don't have an accident or end up in a ditch along the way.

Flying is faster and probably safer but arriving on time isn't guaranteed either. If the snow keeps falling, that flight could be cancelled too, and then what?

Both options validate your value of making it to the wedding, but now you have another set of difficult decisions in front of you.

Neither choice is guaranteed to get you there on time. If the flight is cancelled, that decision is beyond your control. The car, on the other hand, gives you some control, some short-term predictability. If there's a rental available, and it's affordable, you can get on the road in the next hour versus waiting in the airport and hoping the flight out tomorrow will get you there in time. The weather may look moderate, but that's also out of your control, so it's not good information that you can base your decisions on. It's just noise.

In the end, you choose to drive, all night and all the next day. Driving gives you some short-term predictability on how to achieve your goal. Just keep your eyes on the road and plenty of coffee in your cup.

Figuring out your deciding values is the biggest lesson in the messy middle. In the Decision Crisis Playbook, you'll learn how to outline your deciding values and how to assign short-term predictability where you can in order to give yourself the best shot at a good outcome. You'll also learn how to set boundaries—I call them *time and money guardrails*—so you don't end up with any financial or emotional regrets. With guardrails in place, you'll know when it's time to change your plans (pivot) or when it's time to throw in the towel altogether. This is often the hardest part of the Decision Crisis Playbook.

The best news? If you follow the Decision Crisis Playbook, the decisions you make in the messy middle will be good ones. They will be *no-regret decisions*. Decisions that you will be proud of, no matter how things play out in your next normal.

## Phase 3: Your Next Normal

This is the grand reveal! You've made your decision(s) and all of your cards are on the table. Now you get to see how it all pans out. Sometimes this is a celebratory phase of your decision crisis, and sometimes it's not. Either way, this is where you can finally exhale after holding your breath for so long.

If things worked out exactly as you wanted, that's great! It's easy to thrive after a decision crisis when you get 100% of what you wanted or expected. But life is life. Many times, a decision crisis forces you to compromise, to pivot, to give up one thing in exchange for something else. For most of us, our next normal will be a mix of the good rolled in with the bad. But if you're proud of how you made your decisions, then no matter how they play out, you won't have regret. You'll have made the best decisions you could and that will give you confidence in your decision-making ability. That confidence is what will allow you to thrive in your next normal.

During times of transition, when your life is in flux, you don't know what your next normal will look like. But the cool thing is, you have the power to design it right now.

Going back to the wedding scenario: Imagine that you finally left the airport in that rental car at 2 p.m. on Friday. The others in the wedding party all know you're on your way. They're all astounded and delighted and scared and rooting for you. Not knowing the outcome certainly keeps life interesting.

In good weather, you're facing a 20-hour drive (versus a 4-hour flight). The wedding starts at 2 p.m. the next day. After 15 hours of driving (5 a.m. Saturday morning), you have to pull over. It's not safe to continue. You're exhausted, it's still snowing heavily, and it's dark.

You pull over to sleep, set an alarm for 5 hours, and nod off. When your alarm goes off, it's 10 a.m. You wash up in a Starbucks bathroom, brush your teeth, and put on your wedding outfit. You get back in the car and drive the final 5 hours to the wedding. You missed getting ready with the wedding party in the morning. You missed the vows. But at least you made it for the dinner, your speech, and the reception. *Phew!*

Everyone is so happy you are there. They gladly redo a shortened, unofficial, version of their vows over dinner so you can hear them. While you're concerned that you kind of smell because you forgot to buy deodorant, the important thing is you made it. You achieved what matters most to you.

You decide to check if the expensive flight was cancelled. It wasn't. Had you chosen to wait at the airport for the next flight out, you would have made it into town last night. You wouldn't have missed a thing, except some of the rehearsal. *Damn.*

In hindsight (which is always 20/20) that extra $2,000 would have been totally worth it. But you didn't know that at the time. How could you? All flights were cancelled when you made your decision. You knew you couldn't control the weather or airline emergency protocols. You made the best decision for yourself at the time given the information you had and what you knew you could control.

Getting up on the dance floor to join the circle around the bride and groom, you realize you don't care about that flight. You missed the vows but not the wedding. Your friends are happy, you're happy, and you are totally okay with your choice. In fact, it's destined to become one of your all-time favourite stories.

Thriving after a decision crisis is not about being right. It's not about winning or losing. It's about living without regret, so you don't look back and wish you had done something differently.

In this final phase of the Decision Crisis Playbook, you will learn how to embrace your next normal, no matter what the outcome. You'll have hope for the future and, most importantly, the confidence that you can make a good decision again if life throws another lemon your way.

That's often what's so unsettling about a decision crisis. When you find yourself in one, deep down you know that there's no going back to exactly to how things were before. A new version of your life has begun. A next normal is already underway.

The Decision Crisis Playbook steps you through the process of aligning yourself with your deciding values, chasing down any short-term predictability you have, pivoting your plans, and setting guardrails so you don't put yourself at risk or wait too long to make a choice. If you follow the Playbook, you will know that, at the end, you made choices that upheld what's important to you within the constraints of your life. How could you have possibly made another choice?

That being said, there will be times during a crisis when you don't need to work through the entire Playbook. Perhaps you only need to focus on defining your core values, or maybe you need to establish new guardrails because the situation has changed yet again. And then there may be times when all you need is to assure yourself that you have a little control over your situation by going through the short-term versus long-term rating system one more time. The Decision Crisis Playbook isn't a book of rules. It's a book of tools—tools that you'll use again and again, selecting only the ones you need, when you need them.

By the end of this book you will feel confident in your ability to make no-regret decisions and you will be ready for anything—I promise. You *can* make difficult decisions in difficult times, ones that will help you not just survive your decision crisis but thrive when it's over.

# PHASE 1:

## Panic Mode

# CHAPTER 2:

## Getting to 60% Normal

If your decision crisis just started, your daily life probably isn't recognizable, which may be increasing your feelings of panic. You may be mired in thoughts like:

- My whole life just got flipped upside down.
- I miss my old life.
- I don't even recognize my life right now.

Our daily lives consist of rituals and habits. Every day we make many choices. What time should we get up? Should we hit the snooze button? Take a shower? Should we make breakfast or grab fast food on the way to work? What should we wear? Do we need to text anyone a happy birthday meme?

Did we pay the utility bill? All this before 9 a.m. The mental load is exhausting.

That's why we create rituals and routines. It takes the thinking out of so many of our daily choices. This is why people love having automatic bill payments come out of their account and why we do so many of the same things every day. Having to get up, get dressed, brush our teeth, and commute to work is something we do almost automatically. Have you ever arrived at work and been like, *Whoa, I don't even really remember my commute*? (Hopefully you weren't driving.)

The daily rituals in your life are predictable. They are "normal" for you. That's why "normal" feels comfortable. When something interesting or different happens, it's noteworthy because it differs from your normal rituals. When life is unchanged and your routines are intact, you have more headspace to welcome new rituals, practices, and behaviours. But too much change at once can send you into panic mode.

This is the result of something psychologists call "decision fatigue." Many psychologists say that making decisions uses the very same willpower that you use to say no to temptations or to be polite. In other words, it takes work. Effort.

Without daily rituals and routines, you would expend too much of your mental energy and willpower on simple, minute decisions, and your brain would be exhausted before you reached the point in your day when you needed to make really important decisions (maybe about whether you should ask for a raise). When you're mentally exhausted, decisions get shuffled aside, put off until you have more time to think. Sometimes, this means that more difficult choices and decisions never get dealt with at all, and then default outcomes happen, which can lead to regret. Or sometimes you make rash decisions and end up regretting them.

It all comes down to protecting your mental load. That's why Barack Obama, Steve Jobs, and Mark Zuckerberg all famously wore the same outfit and ate the same breakfast every day. They simply didn't want to have to think about that minor stuff. Their morning rituals were as automatic as blinking and required zero mental load.

When you're in a decision crisis, however, your daily rituals and routines are often completely thrown off because your life isn't "normal" anymore. Everything is unpredictable and, therefore, taxing your mental load. If your life just got turned upside down, you haven't created new rituals and routines for yourself yet, so every day is fraught with entirely new decisions.

If you've been laid off, you don't have to wake up, get dressed, brush your teeth, and commute. So what do you do? Do you get up anyways? Get dressed? Apply for jobs? Do you work out? Do you have a second coffee? Go for a walk? Should you call someone? Even these simple self-care decisions take their toll on your overall mental load because things are no longer automatic. You're out of your routine.

You can feel lost without your routines, lacking the mental energy to deal with all the new decisions you need to make. It's exhausting and scary, and if it goes on too long, your ability to achieve a positive outlook can fade.

Self-doubt can set in, leading to apathy, procrastination, and resentment.

The best way to keep moving forward during a decision crisis is to try to reduce not only the number of decisions you need to make in your daily life but also the intensity of the changes around you, which are constant reminders that life is different. You need to make your life feel normal again. Well, *60% normal.*

You can't go back in time, but if you can trick your brain into thinking that some of your "new life" is still "normal," then you'll waste less mental energy each day and preserve some willpower for the bigger decisions that need to be made. That's why finding a way to keep your life 60% normal is important: It gets you out of panic mode for a sustainable longer time. Surrounding yourself with 60% of your existing, pre-crisis daily routines and rituals is comforting and will give you back some mental energy, which will help you move forward to make decisions in the messy middle.

## MEET SUSAN

AGE: 52
RELATIONSHIP STATUS: On the brink of a messy divorce
CHILDREN: 1 (age 20)

A few years ago, my client Susan was in my office because she had just found out that her husband, Kevin, had a gambling problem. A serious one. He had racked up almost

$100,000 of debt on their line of credit and had recently liquidated a portion their retirement savings accounts. All without her knowledge. She was 52 years old with a daughter, Kim, in post-secondary school. In an instant, Susan's current and future life had exploded. Through no fault of her own, she found herself smack in the middle of an external decision crisis.

"I'm so sorry this is happening," I said, noticing that my hand had been on my chest while I was listening to her tell her story.

"Me too." She looked up at me and cleared her throat. "I honestly had no idea. I mean, I thought we were happily married. And we were, or we are. Or—" Her voice caught. She took a sip of tea and shook her head. "I don't know."

"Where are things at right now?" I asked gently.

"I think we are separating? It's all so fresh. I'm living at my sister's place for the time being. Kim, my daughter, is at school and has no idea. I mean, this all just happened a couple of weeks ago."

I nodded. "There's a lot going on right now."

"I feel like my whole life has been turned upside down, and suddenly I have to make so many massive, important decisions for myself and for Kim. If it was just about me, maybe I'd feel differently. But it's not just about me, and I'm absolutely freaking out."

I didn't say anything. This was our very first meeting and I felt like she needed some space to vent.

She took a big breath and let it out slowly. "He's not a bad man." She looked at me earnestly, "I just want you to know that."

I nodded. "Money makes people act in strange ways sometimes."

"The gambling was always a bit of an issue, but it used to be just one or two major sports bets a year, or maybe we'd have a big fight over his losses in a casino a few times a year. I hated it when he gambled, yes, but I never thought it was something that would ruin our marriage or our financial future. I thought it was his . . . recreation. Turns out it was his weakness." She waved a hand. "Or whatever you want to call it."

"How did things progress to where you're at today?"

"Some asshole introduced him to online poker. In hindsight, I now know that was the beginning of the real problem. I didn't realize it at the time, but that was when a major shift happened. When his usual bets worth $1,000 so easily became $10,000 a pop."

"Yikes," I said.

"Yikes is right. We can't afford that kind of thing." She took a long sip of tea. "I feel so stupid because I truly didn't realize where it was headed. When I think back, there were signs. He stayed up late so much more often, well into the night, and was snappy with me more than usual. He'd tell me he lost money or a bet or a game, but he'd lie and say it was $1,000 or maybe $2,000, and I believed him. I never checked our finances." She looked at me. "I'm such a cliché."

"You're not. It's—"

She cut me off. "No, no. I chose not to look at the money. I think in some messed-up way I didn't want to know what he was up to. After his gambling went online, it all went downhill so fast. Everything just spiralled out of control. Within 18 months he had driven up our line of credit to more than six figures and had even taken money out of our retirement accounts."

I saw tears forming in her eyes as she hung her head. I passed her a box of tissues.

"He feels terrible. He's getting help, and he wants to work things out. But I don't know if I can come back from this. I don't know if *we* can come back from this."

"How did you find out?" I asked.

"About a month ago, our bank called to confirm a transfer from our joint retirement account to an old bank account that I didn't realize was still open. I think the banker knew something was going on. Normally, I would have handed the call straight over to Kevin, but he wasn't home." She raised her head and looked at me. "It was a $20,000 withdrawal," she said flatly.

I winced.

She nodded. "Yeah. That's when I knew. Right in that moment."

I let out a long breath. "That is really hard."

"Yes, it is. I have to figure out what I'm going to do next so I can tell Kim what's going on. But every time I start to think about money, Kevin, selling the house . . ." She put her hands over her face. "*Ugh.* I can't even decide what I'm going to make for dinner, let alone make decisions about selling our home or divorcing my husband!"

"Sounds like you're totally overwhelmed. Tell me more about not being able to decide what's for dinner."

"I mean, I eat," she said, almost defensively, "But I just find I'm eating frozen pizza over and over. It requires no effort or decisions, and I can eat it for lunch and dinner and not burden my sister by taking up space in her kitchen. Honestly, any time I think about cooking, it just feels like too much effort. The planning, the cooking, the cleanup. I just want to stare at a wall."

"That makes perfect sense to me. Your life is so incredibly different now. None of your daily routines are the same as they were even 4 weeks ago! That's a lot, Susan."

"It is," she agreed. "It's like I'm living a life that's not mine. I looked in the mirror this morning and actually said out loud to myself, 'Susan, this *is* you. This *is* happening to you.' Like I had to convince myself that this is actually my life. Logically, I know it is, but it doesn't feel at all like my life." Tears fell to her cheeks. She dabbed at them with the tissue. "I still love him, you know? Even after this horrible betrayal."

I nodded.

"And I can't even . . . I just . . . I panic." She barely got the words out.

"I understand."

Susan's life was unrecognizable to her. She had been thrust into an external decision crisis with no time to grieve the loss of her former life and future because she had to think about so many important matters right away, at the worst possible time. She needed to pull herself out of panic mode in order to create hope so she could get in the right headspace to make the decisions that lay ahead of her.

"Sometimes," I said softly, "when there's so much change all at once and you're forced to make a whole bunch of new decisions every day, it becomes too much. You hit decision fatigue, and there's no mental bandwidth left for you to think about, or even recognize, the decisions that matter most. It feels impossible so your brain just shuts down altogether. Like self-preservation."

"Yes, I feel like I'm stuck in the weeds. I can't see the big picture, but I have to find a way so I can make good choices. My brain needs a break."

"*Hmmm.*" I thought for a moment. "I have an idea."

She looked at me, one eyebrow raised. It was the first bit of fun we'd had. "An idea for what?"

"To help give your brain a rest from decision fatigue so you can stop panicking and start making the important decisions you need to make."

She smiled for the first time. "I'm open to anything."

I smiled back at her. "Okay, I want to think about life 4 months ago, in the before times. What did a typical evening look like?"

She sat back. "Well, I guess with Kim away at school, it was pretty normal, pretty quiet. Kevin and I would go to the grocery store or the market and pick up something for dinner, and maybe some wine. We would go back home. I'd listen to music while I cooked, and we'd talk about our day or whatever while we ate. On weekends, I'd go to yoga, we'd have friends over, visit Kim. Nothing wild and crazy."

"Sounds like it was a nice life."

"It was. It really was. That's what makes this so heartbreaking." She sighed. "As I said, the gambling usually happened after I went to sleep."

"So let's focus on the good things for a moment." I had been taking notes the whole time and set the list of daily routines of her life in the before times in front of her.

1. Grocery shopping on a daily basis
2. Treating yourself to a glass of wine
3. Cooking
4. Listening to music
5. Yoga
6. Hosting friends

"Of all the things that were part of normal, daily life," I said, "how many are you still able to do?"

She stared at the page. "None," she said and pushed the list back toward me.

"How come?"

"Because I'm tired and I'm not even at my own house." She grabbed another tissue, dabbed at her eyes, then shook her head as if to snap herself out of her sadness. "Sorry."

"Oh my gosh, please don't be." I took the list back and let a moment of silence pass between us. Then I picked up my pen again and said, "Let's narrow things down a bit. What did a typical morning look like during the work week?"

"Good coffee. Always good coffee." She laughed. "Reading the paper. We kept it old school like that. We'd get ready for work, and then we'd walk to work—rain, snow, or shine. Even if we were bickering, it was still this awesome way for us to connect. We used to joke that our morning commute walk was like date night in reverse. We got our steps in and a vitamin D fix for the day too." She smiled at the memory.

"That sounds lovely," I said. "And you've already mentioned that weekends were about going to yoga, seeing friends, and Kim. Anything else?"

She shrugged. "Maybe some sort of adventure."

"Any of these routines that you didn't like?"

She thought about that. "Well, I used to love drinking wine with Kevin, but alone, right now, it feels different. Because I'm sad. It makes me nervous. I worry about slippery slopes and all that."

I crossed out the wine. "Okay, so here's a list of 10 routines that you still like from your—" I held up my hands to make quotations, "–'old life.'"

1. Grocery shopping on a daily basis
2. ~~Treating yourself to a glass of wine~~
3. Cooking
4. Listening to music
5. Yoga
6. Hosting friends
7. Good coffee
8. Reading the paper in the morning
9. Morning walk
10. Weekend adventure
11. Visits with Kim

I held the pen out to her. "Can you circle the ones that would still give you joy and cross out the ones that either don't bring you joy anymore or that you can't make happen in your current life during this time of transition?"

She pulled the list closer and circled a bunch. We looked at the results together.

| CIRCLED | CROSSED OUT |
| --- | --- |
| Morning walk | Grocery shopping on a daily basis |
| Listening to music | Cooking |
| Yoga | Hosting friends |
| Good coffee | Weekend adventure |
| Reading the paper in the morning | |
| Visits with Kim | |

I pointed to the routines that were scratched out. "Tell me why these four are crossed off."

"I think cooking and grocery shopping will bring me joy again one day, but right now, it's too much." She laughed. "Although I do need a better solution than frozen pizza. Maybe I'll allot myself a high delivery/takeout budget for the next month to make up for all the money I'm not spending doing anything else."

I wrote it down. "That's a great solution. This is your life. You get to decide." I looked back at the list. "What about hosting friends or weekend adventures?"

"I still want those things, but I don't want to see my friends until I know whether I'm going to stay separated from Kevin. And if I am separating, I want to know what the plan is. I'm not sure I want to tell anyone at all if I decide to stay with Kevin. And, I don't feel like doing any sort of adventures right now."

"That's fair. Okay, let's look at the circled ones. These are all routines that make you feel normal and are also within your control. How many of these are you doing right now?"

She laughed. "Not one, actually."

"Not even the coffee?" I asked, faking shock. "How are you surviving?"

She laughed again. "I'm drinking crappy instant coffee at my sister's house. Kevin always made me lattes from our espresso machine. I never learned how to make them."

"I think you need to go get that machine from home. Think you have it in you to learn?" I asked.

"Well, there are online tutorials . . . I really think I must. The bad coffee is adding to my sadness."

"I'm sad just thinking about it," I joked, and we laughed together.

"Okay," I said. "So can I ask you to try the following for the next 2 weeks? Learn how to make good coffee, go to yoga at least once a week, and, every morning, read the paper and go for a walk. I know you're not working right now, but you can still fake a commute."

"That sounds manageable."

"And what about listening to music? How can you build that back in?"

"Easy enough. I'll listen to music on my morning walk. Or podcasts. Podcasts help me escape right now. Also, I just had a thought."

"Go on."

"I really did love cooking. It was a big part of my daily routine. Maybe instead of doing delivery or takeout, I can do those online dinner kits a couple times a week. So that I cook, but I don't have to prep or plan and make a big mess at my sister's place."

"I love that."

"Me too."

"Let's touch base in a couple of weeks and see if you're ready to start making the bigger decisions then."

"I feel less dread right now," she said. "Is that weird?"

"Not at all. I'm basically asking you to make your life as normal as possible. Well, at least 60% normal. Nothing will ever be the same as it was before, but the routines that made up your daily life before meant something to you. They were comforting and didn't take any new willpower. Now, you get to actively pick which ones you're going to take with you through this next part of your journey. *You* get to choose which routines become the rituals that are essential for you to feel like you during this really hard time."

"I like that I get a say in how I want to feel normal again," she said.

"Exactly. These routines are already wired in your brain as part of your normal daily habits. So by adding them back into your life, you're eliminating some of the burden of decision-making. Putting normalcy back into your day will clear up some headspace and also create a ritualistic comfort to get yourself out of panic mode. Then, you can throw some of that brain power toward the bigger, new decisions you need to make regarding Kevin, the house, Kim, etc."

"I get it."

"In essence, using your existing daily routines as rituals will act as very productive and soothing creature comforts."

"I hadn't thought about it like that. But they are comforting. Or, they will be."

She left my office armed with the routines that she would reinstate into her life to get herself to 60% normal. Susan and I had a check-in call 2 weeks later.

"How's it going?" I asked.

"I'm good, actually." And she sounded genuine. "Or as good as I can be."

"Awesome. So how do you feel about your daily life in this moment? Did you manage to get to 60% normal?"

She took her time answering this. "I think so. I've implemented most of the routines we talked about. And I did feel a lighter mental load, almost instantly. But with one exception."

"What's that?"

"The coffee. I lugged the espresso machine to my sister's place, but I just can't figure out the frother."

We laughed.

"So how did you manage to keep your coffee routine?"

"You'll be proud of me. I also budgeted for a takeout latte on my daily morning walk."

"That's great."

"I do feel much calmer than before, and I do believe that getting life to 60% normal has helped a lot. I have a new respect for the mundane in my life."

"*Ohhhh,* I love that."

"Me too. It's like they all became yoga for me."

"What do you mean?" I asked.

"Before all this happened, going to yoga was a routine that eventually transformed into this sort-of ritual. I never missed a class and, if I did, I felt off. The ritual of going to my Sunday-night yoga class really cleared my head and set me up for success for the upcoming week. And now, all of these mundane, boring routines of my old life have taken on the same type of ritualistic importance that yoga used to."

"That's awesome," I said.

"It is, because they are so easy!" She laughed. "Who knew that having coffee and a walk in the morning would become a sort-of sacred self-care ritual? But that's what's giving me hope right now."

"Hope means you're not panicking."

"Exactly!" she said, and I could feel her excitement through the phone. "Is that crazy?"

I smiled. "No. That's exactly what it's supposed to do. It's the perfect way to make you feel safe and free up your headspace."

"60% normal," she said.

"Emotionally close enough to stop the cycle of panic," I explained.

"That's true. I'm still not sure what I'm going to do yet. I am still confused, worried, and mad. But, on a deep level, I know I'll make it through at some point. Or at least that I'm going to survive this without regret."

"That's beautiful. What's giving you that confidence that you won't have regret?"

"Seeing that I can still feel calm even though I'm living at my sister's and my life is completely upside down gives me hope that I can get to a place where I can make the right decisions."

"Let's chat again when you're ready for next steps."

We met in person again 4 months later when she was ready to check in on the bigger plans. We hugged as if we were old friends.

"How are you?" I asked.

"I finally moved back home. It's been a bit of a shitshow, but honestly, we are getting through."

"We?" I asked.

"We," she confirmed. "It's crazy, right? I mean, what kind of person stays with a partner who lied about money and stole from their retirement savings plan?"

I thought carefully about how to respond. "Well, I don't think it's crazy if it's the right decision for you. So the only question I have is: *How do* you *feel about your decision to stay with Kevin?*"

She let out a long breath. "It took a while for me to even be able to put this into words. But trying to work it out and stay in the marriage is the right decision for me right now. I love him and, somehow, I trust that it won't happen again." She scrunched her face, almost waiting for me to judge her.

I didn't judge. "Trust is good."

"Trust is everything," she said. "So he's in addiction counselling, we are in therapy, and I made the decision that the only person I'm telling in my life is, well, you, my sister, and Kim. I don't want to tell any friends or extended family. This is a private family matter, and I just don't want to deal with everyone else's opinions on what's best for me."

"You seem really clear. I'm so glad."

"I am." She went to speak and then stopped for a moment. She looked me right in the eyes. "This is the only shot he gets. Fool me once, that type of thing. If he doesn't uphold his end of our bargain, I'm out and that will be that. On principle. Love or no love."

"That clarity must feel good."

"Very. It's empowering, actually. Once I could finally calm my brain and think about it, I realized that leaving Kevin wasn't the logical decision for me. It would have been a fear-based, panicked decision based on my rage at the betrayal and my fear that my friends and family would judge me or him. Divorce would have been a pride-based, panic-mode decision. One I would have regretted. Once I was able to see that and calmly assess what was important to me, I could bring Kim into the conversation in a rational way without freaking her out or bashing her father. That's my no-regret decision. Now we just have to get our finances back on track so we can put this whole thing behind us and still be okay."

"Hope," I said.

She smiled. "Yes. Hope."

Together, Susan and I made them a new plan. Then she called Kevin to read him the details. He agreed with everything and understood that he would have to work for 5 more years past his original retirement date in order to pay off the gambling debt on the line of credit and replace the money that had been withdrawn from his retirement accounts.

Susan stood up, armed with their new plan, and we hugged. I was so happy that even though she was still in the thick of it, she knew that eventually she'd come out the other side.

By actively choosing which daily routines to incorporate back into her life, Susan had transformed them into comforting rituals that helped lift her out of panic mode and into the next stage of her decision-making process with respect to her relationship and her finances.

Maintaining some of your old rituals is easier than forming new habits. You'll not only be self-soothing, but you'll decrease the decision fatigue that comes when there's too much change happening too quickly in your life.

The best part of 60% normal is that you get to actively choose which routines bring you the most comfort and joy and will accompany you on the journey through your personal crisis, allowing you to ease into the messy middle with hope that you will make the right decisions to take yourself through to the other side.

## HOMEWORK: COMBAT DECISION FATIGUE

**Step 1:** List simple routines you had in your "old normal" or your life before your personal crisis—whatever version of your life felt normal to you. Think mornings, weekdays, evenings, and weekends. Aim for 10. Count them up. The routines can be as simple as "get dressed" or as involved as "go for a hike." Remember: These are routines, not events in your life. Not goals. Simple, almost automatic routines in your life.

**Step 2:** Cross out any routines that are no longer possible for reasons that are out of your control.

**Step 3:** Cross out any routines that, even though possible, aren't serving you during your crisis. Meaning: they make you feel worse, they aren't good for your mental health, or they are counterproductive to your goals. (If you are concerned that you may be implementing routines that are not good for your mental and physical well-being, please reach out to your mental health professional to help you clarify which routines are best for you at this time.)

**Step 4:** Of the routines that are left, circle the ones you want to implement, ones that still give you pleasure and that you feel will serve you best on your journey through your personal crisis.

**Step 5.** Count them up. Does the list reach 60% of the total amount of routines (6 out of 10)? Can you bring 60% of your small, productive, and joyful routines with you through this journey? If you can't get to 60%, that's okay. Do as many as possible for now and revisit the list again next week or next month to see if you can add any more of your daily routines to the list that might be a comforting ritual now.

# CHAPTER 3:

## Creating a Circle of Care

So now that you've reached 60% normal, let's talk about building a circle of care, a step that can make all the difference when you're trying to make decisions in the midst of a crisis. It all starts by finding a circle of people who truly are in the same or similar situation to yours.

In the financial planning world, comparisons happen all the time. I hear things like, "*Ugh*, I don't know how they do that" or "What's wrong with me? If they can afford to do this/that, why can't I?" or "Must be nice for them."

It's natural for humans to compare themselves to others who we *think* are the same as us. Maybe they have the same job as you. Maybe they went to the same school as you. Maybe they live on the same block as you. But the truth is, you don't know if you are the same as someone else. Not really. Not unless you know the nitty-gritty details of their financial lives. Most times, you don't know what's happening behind the scenes financially with anyone. Maybe they married rich. Maybe they are swimming in debt. The point is, you don't know and so you can't compare yourself or your finances.

A comment from a neighbour about how much their house has gone up in value after their renovation can send you into a tailspin if you currently rent. Maybe you want to buy a home one day or maybe you don't. The point is, that comment can make you question *everything*.

Does that mean you're bad with money? Hell, no. Does it mean you should feel insecure about your decision not to buy a home? Definitely not!

Perhaps the reason you decided not to buy was because you don't want to live in the area where you can actually afford a home. Or maybe you're prioritizing other financial goals and buying made no financial sense for you.

I bet if you talked to your relative who rented affordably their whole life, lived where they wanted, and saved a ton of money so they could retire early, you wouldn't feel as scared, insecure, or resentful. Instead, you'd feel inspired, excited, and confident. That's because that person is like you. They get you. They want what you want, and they have similar goals and potentially similar constraints.

The point is, talking about important things with people who want different things than you, have different goals from yours, or have very different resources and constraints than you, isn't helpful. It can make you feel isolated, inadequate, and maybe even resentful.

You need to find *your* people so you can feel understood and validated for the choices you've made and the choices you're about to make. This is true at the best of times. A personal crisis, however, drops you into a very specific type of tough spot, one that magnifies all the negative feelings of being misunderstood, isolated, and lonely. Feeling misunderstood can also lead to bad decision-making: If you think that no one understands you, it can lead you to falsely think you're doing something wrong. Then you start questioning your own values. That's never good. When resentment creeps in, it robs you of your optimism. Without optimism, you start to believe you're bound to fail, your choices become illogical, and you mistakenly believe the only practical step is to leave the path you're on.

When you're in a personal crisis and you've managed to make your life 60% normal, the next thing to do is find your circle of care. Even if it's just one person, the important thing is to connect with someone who gets you. Perhaps a friend or family member. Maybe a professional or someone you've met in an online forum. The point is, they understand *you*. Their tips and advice make sense. You feel heard, supported, properly motivated, and helped.

During the pandemic, many people used the phrase "We are all in the same storm, but in different boats." That's exactly what I'm talking about.

You need to find your boat. You need to seek support from the people in that boat. Why? Because if your boat is sinking and someone comes by on a yacht, no one on the yacht will understand your situation or the choices you made. The advice the people on the yacht give—"Alert the skipper!"—isn't going to help you. The kind of understanding you need only comes from the people in your boat.

## MEET SHIRLEY

AGE: 60

RELATIONSHIP STATUS: Recently widowed

CHILDREN: 2 adult stepchildren and
4 step-grandchildren under age 6

"Shirley, I am so sorry for your loss," I said as I put my hand on hers.

"Thanks," she said, brushing tears away and giving her head a shake. "It's sad, on so many levels."

I nodded. We sat there for a moment in silence, my heart breaking for her.

Shirley is a long-time client of mine. We go way back. Her husband, Peter, had just passed away, suddenly and unexpectedly. Shirley was my client, but her husband hadn't been. In fact, I had never met him.

"We run our finances completely separately," she told me the first time she was in my office. "Second marriage for him, first major commitment for me, but first true love for us both." She gave me a big smile, and it was impossible not to smile back.

Yes, I'm a sucker for a good love story, but there was a warmth to Shirley that always shone through. Her cheerful nature was infectious.

"We both came to the table with money and assets to protect," she explained. "We don't ever want money to come between us. He's much older than me too. So we have lawyers, and pre-nups, and all that jazz. We made the choice together that our house will go to me and the rest of the estate will go to his kids. I'm still planning like I'm single."

At the time of their marriage, she was 45 years old and had done well for herself as a marketing manager. She owned a condo and was about to move in with Peter. But her money was her money, and his was his.

Throughout the years, Shirley checked in with me periodically to ensure that she was on track financially for her eventual retirement. When she was 55, she told me that she wanted to retire at 60.

"So in 5 years?" I'd asked, a little surprised.

She shrugged. "Peter's 70. He's not getting any younger. Plus . . ." She opened up her phone and turned it toward me, revealing a photo of a beautiful, plump baby. "Peter's eldest, Jamie, had a baby last year! I'm a grandma now!"

I beamed at her and the baby. "Oh, Shirley! I'm so happy for you."

"Well, step-grandma," she corrected. "He just turned one. He calls me *Meme*." She stared at the photo. "He's so darn cute!"

"Congratulations."

"Thank you." She closed the phone almost sheepishly. "Although I don't really deserve the congrats. I just got lucky and married a man who came with the whole package. Instant grandma, just add a Peter!"

I knew she was making a joke to deflect some awkwardness. I wondered why.

"I don't think so at all," I said earnestly.

She paused for a moment. "Thanks," she said at last. "I am a bit uncomfortable about it. Am I a grandma just because I'm with Peter? It can be awkward."

"How so?" I asked.

She shifted. "Peter's ex is . . . *Hmmm,* how do I say it nicely? Not a big fan of mine."

I raised an eyebrow. "That's a loaded statement."

"It sure is." She let out a big breath. "I don't like talking trash about the ex, but I will say this: She does *not* make it easy for me."

"Divorce can be one messy beast. Sometimes it makes people act in really strange ways."

She nodded. "That's why I like to give her the benefit of the doubt, you know? She had her heart broken. I can't say I'd be thrilled at the prospect of my grandkids being with another grandma figure if I were in her place."

I nodded.

She waved a hand. "Anyway, the kids live far away. Peter and I really want to be a part of the grandkid's lives, and we've both worked really hard. It's time to start enjoying life."

With that goal in mind, we had made a fairly aggressive savings plan that would let her fully retire and step into the role of *Meme.*

That was 5 years ago. Over that time, Shirley stuck to the plan, hit all of her savings goals, and had recently celebrated her 60th birthday. She was on track to retire early, but suddenly a huge part of the plan was missing. Peter.

"When did he pass?" I asked.

She lowered her eyes. "Eight weeks ago."

"I really am sorry, Shirley."

I knew money wasn't the issue. Shirley was set for retirement, and we had always planned on her retirement being entirely funded by her own efforts.

Tears spilled onto her cheeks and she grabbed a tissue. "I'm not only dealing with the loss of Peter, which is devastating enough." She blotted her face. "It's the fear of losing the grandkids too."

"What do you mean?"

"Peter's ex still doesn't like me," she said softly. "Over the years she's tried to convince some of the kids, the adult kids, that I'm not a good person or something. I'm worried that with Peter gone, and the fact that they live over an hour away from us . . . me . . . but super close to her, I'll never see them again. It was always Peter who made the family community happen. I'm not close enough with the adult kids to demand a visit, you know? I'm not sure if they even really like me. I think so, but it's hard to tell. I probably won't even see them at Christmas anymore."

Tears fell.

"That is a whole extra layer of complexity added to your grief."

"It sure is," she said between sniffs.

"Have you tried to talk to them about it?"

She shook her head. "I'm too scared. I don't want to tick anybody off or seem like I'm not grieving Peter, and I still have to work with them to settle the estate." She blew her nose. "I just don't know what to do. I don't know what's the right way. I can't even think straight. Trying to be logical while grieving is impossible. I just wish someone had a rule book for this, you know?"

I nodded. "That would be helpful."

"Anyways, sorry for unloading all of this on you when we are supposed to be running numbers on my condo, not blubbering and venting about my family life."

"Actually, that's exactly what I'm here for," I said. "Vent away."

"It feels good to talk honestly about this."

"I bet."

"It's just that all my friends are still married with blood-relative grandkids or they are single for life with no kids. Either way, they don't understand."

"How so?"

"Obviously, everyone is wonderful and I shouldn't be talking like this. They are all doing their best–"

I interrupted her. "Shirley, stop trying to be nice for one second. I don't know any of the people you're talking about, and I couldn't tell them anything you say to me even if I tried. Just speak bluntly."

She slumped back in the chair. "It's like I can't stand talking to my friends right now, which makes me so mad at myself and so sad."

"What's happening when you speak with your friends?"

"Well, the ones who are married with blood-relative grandkids are so optimistic that I can't stand talking to them. They tell me to be positive and that the relationship with the grandkids will shine through no matter what. But they don't understand the complexities of being a step-grandparent without the blood-relative connection, especially if an ex-wife hates you and constantly tarnishes your name to the adult kids."

I nodded and waited for her to keep going.

"And many of my single friends who never married say that even if I never see my step-grandkids again, I should be grateful for the time I had." She threw her hands up in exasperation. "I feel like I have to watch my words at all times so people don't think I'm nasty or that I'm unappreciative or that I don't miss Peter. All I care about is the grandchildren. I'm obviously devastated about everything, but I feel like I can't be sad in the way I want to be sad or worried about the things I'm worried about." She shook her head. "I'm tired, but I can't get my brain off this. I keep going around and around, and I keep procrastinating when it comes to settling the estate."

"I can't imagine how tough this must be."

"Plus, this is all I want to talk about right now, and at some point, people get tired of hearing the same thing over and over with no action."

"That sounds lonely."

"That's exactly it. I feel lonely even though I'm surrounded by community. My community is wonderful but just not a good fit right now."

"Do you know anyone in a similar situation to you?"

"Widowers of second marriages with complex exes?" She gave one of those loud laugh-cries.

I laughed too. "Sounds about right."

"What an extremely specific support group that would be."

An extremely niche support group, indeed. But worth a shot.

"Shirley, I think that's your answer."

"How so?"

"When I listen to you, you feel like no one understands. You're lonely and don't know what to do next, which is making you spiral and panic. Who better to help you than people who are in the same situation or who have lived through the same situation? Like a circle of care."

"That's a good point." She paused. "But where would I find this group? Craigslist personal ads?"

I had always loved her sense of humour.

"Let's brainstorm some people who may know someone you can get in touch with."

We made a list of places. When we were done, she was going reach out to three people to ask if they knew someone in a similar situation and ask if they were okay with being connected.

1. Her lawyer
2. An anonymous (to start) post in an online divorce community
3. Her therapist

We knew privacy laws wouldn't allow either her lawyer or therapist to give out names, but they might be able to point her in a new direction or to support groups.

"Keep me posted," I said.

It was only 3 weeks later when I heard from Shirley regarding the support groups.

"I wanted to say thank you," she said.

"So what happened?" I asked.

"The online divorce community came through. I asked the administrator to post anonymously, specifically asking for women who were not in first marriages and had step-grandchildren."

"And . . . ?"

"I was actually really nervous and excited when I saw other women commenting on the post. I wanted to shout, "I'm not alone!'"

"Tell me about them."

"There were four women who posted. Two are going through it right now just like me. Their husbands died within the last 6 to 12 months. The other two had this happen to them a few years ago."

"Did you connect with any of them?" I asked.

"Yes, and I asked them all if they wanted to join a group chat together, and they did. We started a Second Wives Club." She smiled. "Oddly enough, Widowers of Second Marriages with Complex Exes was taken."

I laughed. "So how has this extremely niche chat group helped?"

"We sort of have an ongoing conversation every day. Sometimes really deep and profound emotional conversations and sometimes it's a funny internet joke or a helpful article link. It feels like a really safe space to blow off steam with people who get it."

"That's wonderful."

"It's only been 3 weeks, but I feel closer to these women than I have felt with some of my other friends during this whole thing. Grief bonding. Shared experience. I feel like I can be myself."

"You feel seen."

"Yes. And understood."

"When do you lean on this group the most?"

"It helps to give me a safe sounding board if I'm panicking or spiralling or I just need to cry. Also, the two women who have been dealing with this for a while have given me some really helpful tips on how to manage the step-grandkid thing and the fragile politics around it. Plus, they helped me come up with some helpful communication strategies so I don't get cut off from visits. It's only been 3 weeks, but I've started to bridge the gap, and I'm seeing the kids for the first time since the funeral tomorrow."

My heart lightened at the smile on her face. "I'm so glad."

"Me too. I'm really leaning on this group for support right now, which is also helping my other friendships. I get that my friends don't want to sit and overanalyze an email from my stepson for an hour. That's okay. Because I'm getting that support with the group, I don't need that from my usual friends. It was probably unfair of me to expect that of them."

"I'm so happy you found this circle of care," I said.

She nodded. "It's given me hope that there will come a day when I don't cry, and that's a good feeling. I have hope again."

When you're in a personal crisis, you need to surround yourself with other people who are in the same/similar circumstances as you. This will make you feel seen, heard, and understood—a critical step to keep you from feeling isolated. Having a sounding board of people who get you and don't make you feel like you can't be you allows you to relax and be honest with them and yourself. Plus, you'll get helpful advice, strategies, and information from the group of people who share what's important to you. This is the importance of community, assuring you that you're not alone while you go through this.

## HOMEWORK: CREATE A CIRCLE OF CARE

**Step 1:** Define your specific situation. What is unique about your goals? What's unique about your constraints and your needs right now in your crisis?

**Step 2:** Find people in similar situations who can meet up, hang out, talk. Is it a support group? Is there an online community?

**Step 3:** Make a list of personal and professional contacts who can help you connect with others in your same circumstances.

People who are going through the same things understand where you are and what you're feeling. Do you think your neighbour may be experiencing the same thing? A pal who went through a similar situation years ago?

**Step 4:** Reach out. This is the hard part. Tell them what you're going through and be specific that you're looking to chat with someone who has gone through a similar experience.

**Step 5:** Ask if they are willing to be in your circle of care as you journey through this crisis. Are they okay to give you space to be you?

**Step 6:** If they agree, create a reoccurring communication with them so you can use them as a sounding board or person to vent with.

*Remember:* This could be one person, an entire online community, a neighbour, an existing support group of friends, your therapist, even your accountant! Whoever makes you feel seen, heard, understood, and can offer helpful guidance and support.

# CHAPTER 4:

## Using Micro Timelines and Micro Goals for Damage Control and Forward Movement

Now that you've achieved 60% normal and created a circle of care, it's time to implement what I call *micro timelines* and *micro goals* to keep you moving forward.

Uncertainty is part of life, and no one has a crystal ball, but in times of crisis, uncertainty feels different, heavier. And the higher the stakes, whether emotional or financial, the more frightening uncertainty becomes, keeping you mired in panic mode. Panic can make you want to spring into action, to do something, *anything*, but it may not be time yet.

We know that the best way to break out of panic mode is to feel both safe and happy at the same time, a combination that provides you with short-term hope. However brief, that optimism should be enough for you to give your head a shake and access that rational part of your brain that says, "You're safe right now. Everything will be okay."

Micro timelines with micro goals allow you to pull yourself out of panic mode and keep putting one foot in front of the other. They allow you to buy yourself time for the really important decisions without making your situation worse, all while taking small but meaningful steps to give yourself purpose and promote hope.

With so much uncertainty and changing information during a personal crisis, creating a list of small, manageable tasks on a 4-hour, 4-day, 4-week basis gives you back control and ensures that you're taking positive action to promote a growth-oriented outlook, even while you're still in the thick of it.

As a financial planner, I'm expected to tell people that "it all starts with a plan" and that "the financial plan will save you." This is true to a degree, but long-term financial planning doesn't always fit the bill.

In the old-school ways of financial planning, your financial plan would be a 40-page document outlining your retirement projections. It added up everything you planned to save over your lifetime and directed exactly how you would take your money out in retirement, in a tax-efficient manner. The plan gave you a snapshot of what your cash flow would look like in your golden years.

The point of the plan was to provide comfort. "You're safe. Do this and everything will be okay." That's pretty dreamy, yet I always questioned the logic.

Suppose you are 45 years old and your retirement plan meant you had to save $8,000 a year until age 65. But at age 48, you unexpectedly become a caregiver for an aging parent and your expenses go up by $3,000 a year. Now, you can only save $5,000 a year toward retirement. This decrease in saving doesn't align with *the plan*. So what now? Are you screwed? Should you worry? Will you be okay?

Suddenly, you feel like your whole future has been thrown off course and you may never recover. What if you can't retire at all? The list of what-ifs grows, fear takes over, and panic sets in, potentially plunging you straight into a personal crisis. If you can't even stick to your financial plan, you must be bad with money. If you're bad with money, how can you make sound decisions? If you can't make sound decisions, what's the point in trying? Maybe you should just throw in the towel and forget the whole thing. This kind of fatalistic thinking happens all the time when our plans go awry.

Logic says that none of that is true, but in the midst of a crisis, logic doesn't always make an appearance. All you know is that you've failed at *the plan*. You've let yourself down. But the reality is that those long-range plans aren't realistic most of the time. They usually only work when someone is a few years away from retirement. Even then, every plan needs flexibility.

Your projected plan is only as good as the data that goes into it. Data that is nothing more than assumptions about how your life will play out, and therein lies the problem. Life has a way of messing with the best-laid plans.

The good news is that short-term plans are super useful and super helpful.

I'm not saying those long-term plans are useless. They help, but they aren't great at showing you how to execute over the short term. Whenever I'm making a financial plan, I look at my client's financial life as a road trip.

Let's think of retirement as your final destination on a road trip across Canada, starting in St. John's, Newfoundland (you now) and ending in Victoria, B.C. (happily retired). Maybe Ontario is where you buy a home or realize that renting is what you prefer. Maybe Saskatchewan is where you have babies or raise dogs.

No matter what you envision at each stage along the way, a typical 40-page comprehensive financial plan will simply draw the most efficient route from Newfoundland to Victoria across a map of Canada. Sounds good in theory, but what if you get a flat tire (lose your job) in New Brunswick? Or end up on a detour (quit your job to start your own business) in Manitoba? Long-term plans leave no room for bumps in the road or detours of any kind. If you're off course, you've failed.

Short-term planning, on the other hand, looks at the big map and creates a rough itinerary for the trip from start to finish. Yes, it asks you to think about what you might do in each province and how many kilometres you should be averaging a day to ensure you get to Victoria by your desired time. But the real focus is the short-term timeline. The section of road directly in front of you, not the one two provinces away. You'll think about those as you get closer to them. For now, what's in front of you is enough. It's the only part that's reasonably predictable and that's key.

A short-term plan also helps keep you motivated and, perhaps most importantly, it gives you back some control. It's daunting to look at the whole journey from Newfoundland to B.C., but if you focus only on getting out of St. John's by nightfall, it's much more manageable. Even if it's raining, you can predict that and shift your actions accordingly, which can be very comforting.

I use short-term timelines to create control, predictability, and a feeling of security at the best of times. But when clients are in crisis, I go one step further and use *micro timelines* and *micro goals*.

Micro timelines are like short-term timelines on steroids and are critical to providing a framework for damage control in any emergency that requires you to make decisions quickly. Micro goals are the actions you can take within a micro timeline to move yourself forward when making plans or decisions in the midst of a personal crisis.

While you're in a crisis, there are some things you need to deal with right away and others that you need to hold off on until there is more information, more clarity, etc. Deciding too soon can put your long-term core values and goals at risk. You can't do it all. You can't know it all. Micro timelines give you permission to deal with short-term emergencies with short-term solutions. These solutions may not be ideal over the long run, but you can always return to the larger, longer-term issues later, after the crisis passes.

Taking meaningful action, even in the extremely short run, can restore your sense of control and reduce anxiety. Some action means less panic and a sense of accomplishment.

Micro goals are small actions you can take to regain control over the course of your micro timeline while ensuring your core values remain at the centre of the plan. What are core values? They're the things that matter most to you on an emotional or spiritual level. They make up the standard or code by which you live. So any plan that does not take those values into consideration is doomed to fail.

Not only identifying your core values but writing them down, seeing the words on a page or a screen, is an important step to setting micro goals and micro timelines that will work for you.

With so much uncertainty during a decision crisis, you may not be able to tackle the greater issues exactly how or when you'd like to. Imagine you are getting divorced and the mounting anxieties you would feel over what will happen to the matrimonial home. Will you have to move? Where will you move? How much spousal support/child support will you receive or have to pay? Which of your core values are top of mind?

There are so many unknowns, it can be overwhelming. So much is beyond your control, and you feel like you may be spinning your wheels. Micro goals allow you to say, "I can't do anything to control the child support or where I'm going to live in this moment, but I *can* control what happens to me in the next 24 hours. I *can* make some micro decisions today."

When a crisis hits, you need to narrow your focus. Plan only for the few metres directly in front of you, the part of the journey you *can* control at the moment. It's too early to worry about what's over the next hill. By focusing on the extreme short run, you can combat any emergency situations, implement damage control, and start to make some plans that give you a sense of control. When you feel in control of even a small part of your life, it restores your faith in yourself, assuring you that you will have the capacity for reliable, no-regret decisions at some point, and doing minimal damage to your circumstances in the short run while you wait for more information.

## MEET CLINT

AGE: 48

RELATIONSHIP STATUS: Committed (about to move in together)

CHILDREN: None

Clint was one of the hundreds of clients I worked with over the duration of Canada's first lockdown in early 2020. He was a travel agent and having a hard time. Not only had he been laid off recently, the tenants in his rental condo had just given him notice that they would be moving out in 30 days. Clint didn't own the home where he lived. His rental property was his major real-estate asset.

"I'm so sorry this is all happening," I said.

He held up his hands then let them fall. "I feel so unprepared. I never imagined anything like this. The rental property was supposed to be the ace up my sleeve, diversifying my income so I wasn't just relying on my job. I never thought I'd lose both in one week."

"This pandemic is totally unprecedented in our lifetime."

"My realtor says I could probably offload the condo relatively quickly but at a loss. My girlfriend thinks I'm an idiot to sell. I did try to get new tenants, but no one wants to rent the condo at the same price as before, so it's vacant right now. I'm going to lose money every month on the condo." He tipped his head back, stared at the ceiling a moment, and then let out a massive sigh. "I feel like I'm losing no matter what right now."

"That's a lot of pressure."

"It is. You always tell me that my future income stream is my greatest asset, right?"

I winced. "Yes, but—"

"Exactly. I have no rental income, I have no job, and my industry is probably gone forever since no one will travel for years, and maybe never again the way they used to, and my girlfriend is probably not going to move in with me now."

He was talking so fast it was almost hard to keep up. The job loss combined with 30 days' notice from the tenant had pushed Clint into an external decision crisis and his panic was evident.

"I need to retrain or see a career coach as fast as possible," he said. "I don't even care what I do, anything that can be done remotely and isn't about large crowds and travel. And the longer I do nothing, the worse it gets. I need to do something, like yesterday."

I took a long pause. On purpose. I wanted to slow us down. "Okay, I hear you. I'm going to ask you a strange question. I want you to tell me what's at stake here."

"What do you mean?"

"I mean, you're talking quickly, your breath is shallow, you're obviously really worked up. People don't get this worked up unless something really important is on the line. What exactly is on the line for you right now?"

"Money. Obviously."

"The lack of it coming in."

"Yes. I have no money coming in and all of these major decisions. Do I sell the condo? Do I keep it and take the loss? I want Lyndsey to move in with me, and I don't want to be stupid about money."

It was good to get to the heart of it.

"Tell me what you mean about being stupid with money."

"Instead of making money and saving for the future, I'm now facing a massive financial shortfall every month and I'm using my line of credit to cover it. If I stay in my rental apartment and hang on to the condo without it being rented, I lose. If I sell and take a massive hit on the price, I lose. Either way, I'm screwed." He put his head in his hands. "I should have done something differently."

Regret and self-recrimination, two things that often rear their ugly heads during a crisis.

"How does Lyndsey moving in factor into this?" I asked.

He kept his head down. "We are in totally different camps on this whole financial thing. We just aren't seeing eye to eye. She thinks we should live in the condo. I have never wanted to live there. I like my neighbourhood. That's where I want to be. We got into a massive fight this morning, and she said that maybe she doesn't want to move in at all now. This pandemic is making every decision feel, I dunno, not normal."

Poor guy. It was clear to me that he was facing two distinct emergency situations:

1. Racking up his line of credit to pay for the condo, his apartment, and his day-to-day life.
2. Fighting with his partner about money/moving in.

We needed damage control.

In a decision crisis, there are some decisions that need to be put off. You should wait until you're in the right headspace to make important no-regret decisions with enough good information to make that decision. You need time to gather that information so you don't make panicked, irrational decisions. The problem is, there are also times when waiting even a few days will make your situation astronomically worse.

Think about having to decide whether or not to apply for a job.

You find a job post that looks good. There's a lot of unknowns. You're not sure it's a good fit, but there's a deadline. It's tomorrow. Even if you're still conflicted and panicked, you still have to act. If you don't, you'll miss that deadline and the cost of doing nothing may come back to bite you later.

Even while in panic mode, sometimes the cost of doing nothing outweighs the cost of waiting until you have the right outlook and information. Often you can't get out of panic mode until you've dealt with the emergency right in front of you. This is damage control. And it's why you need a micro timeline and micro goals. Sometimes you just need to stop the bleeding.

I had to find out if we were in a damage control situation with Clint.

"Can you tell me how much the monthly shortfall is?"

He shook his head. "I dunno. A lot. I have no tenant. I had to cover my own rent with my line of credit last week. And now I have no paycheque coming in to pay it back. Do I just need to sell it? I'm freaking out."

"It's okay. You've got this. Let's start with the shortfall."

We ran the numbers for the condo. He used to rent it for $2,700. Without a tenant, the mortgage, taxes, and maintenance fees would put Clint $2,000 in the hole each month on the condo. That was a lot but not insurmountable if this arrangement was only for an extremely short period of time. I needed to help him see some light in his tunnel.

"The carrying costs for the condo aren't all that high for a city property. It was very profitable until just recently."

"Yeah, it was a great property before all this. It's my retirement plan. Or was."

This was a perfect example of panic forcing trade-off thinking. Black-and-white choices.

He owned a property that, up until a completely unprecedented global pandemic, had been cash-flow positive. It had a low mortgage, was in a great location, and diversified his portfolio as well as ensuring that he would always have a place to live in retirement if he needed to. So smart. It had only been a few days since the tenants gave him their last rent cheque. Selling or holding on to the condo was not a decision to be made in panic mode. He needed to be in a better frame of mind and needed much more information before deciding the fate of that condo. He needed to buy himself some time. However, he was actively sinking into debt and a solution for that had to be dealt with ASAP.

"Do you really want to sell it?" I asked.

He groaned. "I just want to make a smart move."

"What will a smart move give you?"

"Peace of mind. That way I can assure Lyndsey that I have a plan and I'm not an idiot."

I asked him to list all the major life decisions he had to make during this time of crisis.

"I need to decide if I'm selling the condo or moving into the condo. I need to figure out if I need to retrain for a new career or apply for new jobs."

I shared my screen with him and started typing into a document.

## DECISIONS NEEDED

- Do I sell the condo?
- Do I move into the condo?
- Do I retrain?
- Do I get a new job?

Then I asked him what the motivation was behind each decision.

"What do you mean?" he asked.

"Why is it important for you to make these choices?"

"Well, I am losing $2,000 a month on the condo while it's vacant. If I can't get a tenant soon, I need to either sell it or move into it."

"What about the re-training?"

He shrugged. "I need to get a job so I can pay my bills."

| DECISION | SHORT-TERM MOTIVATION |
|---|---|
| Do I sell the condo? | Save money on the mortgage and carrying costs |
| Do I move into the condo? | Eliminate expenses for current apartment |
| Do I retrain? | New skills for a world that may not need travel agents after the pandemic |
| Do I get a new job? | Cover current expenses without selling or moving |

"These all feel like short-term, panic-based motivations, not necessarily your long-term core values," I said.

"I don't get it."

"In a normal situation, re-training or getting a new job wouldn't just be about covering your expenses or not losing money. Correct me if I'm wrong, but if you weren't in crisis right now, other things would likely come into play when thinking about changing careers or looking for a new job. Things like enjoyment, opportunities, a different workplace culture, etc."

"Oh yeah, for sure."

"If you weren't in crisis right now, what would be that bigger, long-term motivation for you to switch jobs or careers? Think about the last time you applied for a job. What were you hoping for?"

He thought about this. "I didn't want to hate my job. But ultimately, it was about being able to save some money for retirement. My parents had nothing. I don't want to end up like that."

"Okay. So, ultimately, future financial security is what's at stake for you when making job search and re-training decisions."

He nodded in agreement.

"What about the condo? Moving in or selling it. What was the reason you bought that particular condo, before you were in crisis?"

"It's in a nice area, near the subway. I figured it would rent easily. I always hoped that the rental income would provide a sort of quasi-pension for me in retirement, because I prefer living in a rented accommodation. Buying the condo was a way to have some real estate without it being my primary residence."

"So again, I'm hearing that long-term or future financial security is the major concern if you weren't in a crisis."

"For sure."

I typed that into the chart so he could see.

| DECISION | SHORT-TERM MOTIVATION | LONG-TERM VALUES |
|---|---|---|
| Do I sell the condo? | Save money on the mortgage and carrying costs but lose potential for future rental income | Long-term financial security |
| Do I move into the condo? | Eliminate expenses for current apartment; lose potential for future rental income | Long-term financial security |
| Do I retrain? | Cover expenses | Long-term financial security |
| Do I get a new job? | Cover expenses | Long-term financial security |

"To me, your situation reads as a short-term emergency," I said. "This doesn't sound like the time to decide between selling or not selling, re-training or not re-training. This is the time for damage control, including micro timelines and micro goals."

"*Hmmm.* I hadn't thought about it like that."

"If we can find a way to stop the financial bleeding for a little while, that will buy us some time on the sell/no sell/move in/re-training decisions you have to make."

"But if I don't act now and wait until I get a tenant, I'll still be floating all this money on my own."

"We need to generate some short-term damage control options, including micro timelines and goals. These solutions aren't necessarily ideal for the long run, but without them the short-term costs can be high." I sat back, giving him a moment to process that information, then I asked, "What does your gut instinct say about your chances of getting new tenants or bringing in more money?"

He let out a big sigh. "Maybe if I offered a lower rental price, say $2,400 a month, I could maybe get someone in there by next month."

"Well, you could go as low as $2,000 and still break even. So $2,400 would still have you making money each month. So let's start with a micro-timeline plan. There are a lot of things beyond your control right now and a lot of information needed before making those bigger decisions. We need to do some damage control to give you some immediate peace of mind. But instead of trying to solve all your problems over the next 4 months to 4 years, let's just focus on the next 4 weeks. A micro timeline."

"Four weeks?" he said.

"Yep."

He thought about this. "Shouldn't I be seizing the day and taking action?"

I went back to his short-term/long-term motivation chart.

"Do you think that buying time and waiting 4 weeks will give you a chance to get more useful information in order to make a good decision about selling the condo or moving in?"

He thought. "Yes, because if I can rent it to someone, I don't have to worry about losing money every month. And then I can weigh the pros and cons of selling during a pandemic."

"I agree," I said and added it to his list. "What about re-training? Do you think buying time and reassessing in 4 weeks will give you an opportunity to get better information that will allow you to make a better decision?"

"For sure. I don't even know what I want to do or how I'd pay for school."

I wrote that down too.

"Lastly, what about finding a new job? Do you feel like waiting to take action here will give you a better chance at making a decision?"

He thought. "No. I don't actually. Who knows how long this will go on? Right now, I think I need to start applying for jobs I'm good at and already trained for."

I nodded and added that to the chart (see chart on p. 86).

Again, I shared my screen with him so he could see.

"The only thing you need to do right now is set some micro goals for those short-term high stakes. Start applying for jobs and buy yourself some time to get clarity on the condo and the re-training."

"But what about after 4 weeks?" he said.

"Who cares about what happens after that? Everything could change again at any moment. Maybe the pandemic

| DECISION | SHORT-TERM STAKES | LONG-TERM STAKES | WILL BUYING TIME GIVE YOU BETTER INFO? |
|---|---|---|---|
| Do I sell the condo? | Sell at a loss and lose potential for $2,000/ month rent | Financial security | Yes |
| Do I move into the condo? | Eliminate expenses for current apartment; lose potential for $2,000/ month rent | Financial security | Yes |
| Do I retrain? | Cover expenses | Financial security | Yes |
| Do I get a new job? | Cover expenses | Financial security | No |

will be over, maybe you'll have a tenant willing to pay $2,700, maybe $2,400. Who knows? The point is we can only predict your life for the next 4 weeks. During that time, we stop as much financial damage as possible so that you don't make a panicked decision that will impact your long-term stakes."

We looked at his bank accounts and then we went through and mapped out any income he could expect from government programs. Our next step was to list all expenses, including the condo, that were due.

When we were finished, we knew he'd be looking at a $2,500 deficit each month. In 4 weeks from today there would be an additional $2,500 on the line of credit. He looked defeated.

"I'm looking at your expenses," I said. "You've already cut it pretty tight. You don't live extravagantly."

"I don't. But what more can I do?"

"Okay, I'm not normally a fan of slashing expenses or," I lowered my chin and put on my best wrestling-announcer voice, "*extreme budgets* because they set people up for failure over the long run. But if we are only talking 4 weeks, and it's an emergency, I can get behind it."

"So what do I do?"

"Are there any expenses here that you feel could come down, even if it's to an unsustainably low amount, without putting your health or safety at risk for the next 4 weeks?"

He scanned his expenses. "The subscriptions for sure. I can always autostart them again next month if things change."

"Great." Seventy dollars saved.

"And I can live on a shoestring for the next 4 weeks."

We reduced his variable spending money down to $500 for the next month, saving $430 a month. "I know $500 for spending money is much lower than what you're used to, but this is not forever. This is just for now until the tenant situation is dealt with."

He took a deep breath. "I know."

"Okay, you'll save $500 a month so you're only going into debt by an additional $2,000 while you have no tenant for the next 4 weeks."

"And that's good?"

"Well, it's better than $2,500. And remember, this is a micro timeline. This isn't your life. This is just for now. By doing this, it means that the government programs you'll apply for will cover your life expenses. That's huge. Now, any additional debt will come strictly from the condo. If you manage to get a tenant in there at $2,400, you'll profit by about $300 (after-tax) and you'll be able to pay back the $2,000 in 8 months. Then you'll be back in a cash-flow-positive position again."

"What if I don't get a tenant in 4 weeks?" he said.

"If this goes on, it will be 3 months before you'd be maxed out on your line of credit. That $7,500 ($6,000 new debt and $1,500 from paying rent after job loss) would take a long time to pay back. I think if you can't get a tenant in 3 months, other options and levers will have to be pulled. If you sold the condo, you would pay off the line of credit with the proceeds of the sale. Even though you'd be selling it at a lower price than you hoped for, your mortgage is really low. There's still equity there, even after you pay taxes."

He let out a big sigh.

"Is that relief?" I asked.

"I think so," he said cautiously. "It's weird. I thought the micro goal would be to stop debt altogether and sell the condo or move into it."

"That's an extreme take. I prefer finding an emotional and financial win that will last beyond 4 weeks. A snap decision now could likely lead to regret later. There are just too many unknowns right now, and it doesn't sound like you're even sure you want to sell. A 4-week micro timeline coupled with a profound reduction in your living expenses and a reduction in rent on the condo to tempt a tenant to move in quickly gives us a micro goal with a degree of predictability. It's financial harm reduction that gives you a moment to come out of panic mode, ensuring that the bigger decisions are the ones you truly want to make."

"Mic drop," he said.

I laughed.

"At the end of 4 weeks, we will reconvene. We will know so much more by that point and can make decisions that are totally different from the ones you are making today. When we meet in 4 weeks, there will be another $2,000 on your line of credit, but that is part of the plan."

"I guess I can tell Lyndsey that."

"Totally. Let her know that you're working on a micro timeline with micro goals. That you're going to try to find a tenant at a reduced but still profitable rent over the next 4 weeks and that we will reconvene then. Let her know that you have a hard stop at 3 months. Then you'll either move into the condo or sell it."

"I'll talk to her tonight."

"Good."

He gave his head a shake. "My life is so crazy right now."

"It is." I confirmed. "But it's not forever. It's just for now."

"For sure, and this has really helped me feel better about it. Like, I know that I can at least make it until the end of the month, and I have a plan for it."

When we met 4 weeks later, Clint still hadn't found a tenant, but he had talked it out with Lyndsey. She was totally on board with the plan. They would give it a go for 3 months total in their controlled way. They wanted to hold out for $2,400 rent, keep trying to find a tenant, and then make the bigger decisions later on.

Knowing that he was supposed to be another $2,000 in debt after 4 weeks had given him permission to do it without guilt or worry. He didn't feel like a financial failure. He was exactly where he was supposed to be on his micro timeline, giving him some much-needed control and predictability, making it possible to pull himself out of panic mode.

Micro timelines worked really well for Clint. He felt confident he wasn't making things worse by buying himself some time to make bigger life decisions later.

By taking a few, albeit extreme, temporary measures to cut expenses, Clint knew he was doing minimal financial damage in the short term, which made him feel safe.

"I'm still freaking out," he said with a slight laugh. "I feel good about the damage control plan. I'm still on board. I cut the expenses that I said I would cut, and I'm trying to get a tenant for $2,400, but I feel like I'm . . ." He stopped to think about what he wanted to say next and then let out a sigh. "I feel like I'm pacing."

He wasn't actually pacing. I could see that he was seated at his desk. But I knew what he meant.

I smiled. "Sometimes, when I feel anxious about outcomes that have so much uncertainty and massive stakes, I pace too. I often say I feel like a puppy who wants to go outside but it's too cold, so I just run around and around in circles, barking."

"I feel like that for sure," he said.

"Okay, I'm going to give you some homework."

He drew his head back. "What? More?" he asked with a laugh.

"Well, you called me for a reason!" I smiled. "Don't be scared. I'm just going to give you something to keep you busy right now while you wait for the rest of the cards to fall."

"I don't want to do busy work. I need to do something that is going to help me get out of this situation."

"Which is exactly what this will do. I call it the *safe and happy grid*."

I shared my screen and opened up Excel. (I friggin' love spreadsheets!)

In one column I wrote *Scared/Anxious.*

"What's making you feel scared or anxious right now?" I asked.

"Oh, let me count the ways," he joked, then rhymed them off like a laundry list. "I have no money coming in. I'm worried my girlfriend thinks she can't count on me. My industry may not exist ever again. There's a pandemic. I have no tenant. I don't know if I could even get a job right now." He shrugged and smiled. "I think that's about it."

I nodded and pointed to the screen with my cursor. "Okay. So let's break these down." I started with the line *No money coming in.* "What's one action you can do in the next 4 weeks to appease this fear?"

He thought for a moment. "I can make sure I've applied to all the new government programs. Maybe see a career coach or something? And I can keep making those budget cuts we talked about."

I smiled. Three actions. A good sign.

I indicated the next line on the chart. "What's going on with being worried that Lyndsey can't count on you?"

He looked down at his desk. "Those are my words. We've never actually had a hard conversation. I'm just worried she's worried. We are so at odds with how this pandemic will play out financially for everyone. I don't want to make the wrong choices. As an earner, or provider or whatever stereotypical, gross thing I'm feeling right now."

"What do you mean?"

He let out a long sigh. "We talk about having kids in the next 5 years, and with all this financial upheaval, I don't want her to lose faith in me."

"So, in the next 4 weeks, what's one action that you could take to appease this anxiety?"

"I just really need to talk to Lyndsey about all of this. I have been avoiding it because I want to wait to show her that I can get a tenant and we don't have to sell or move."

"How do you plan on talking it through with her?" I asked.

"Maybe I should just show her the 4-week plan we made? See if she can buy into it with me. Understand that we don't have all the information we need right now but would likely regret a panic-based decision."

I typed it into the list.

We went through the rest of the Scared/Anxious list line by line, determining what small actions he could take in the next 4 weeks to appease his fear or anxiety. Here's what he came up with:

| SCARED/ANXIOUS | MICRO GOALS |
| --- | --- |
| I have no money coming in to cover rent, mortgage, and regular expenses | Apply to government income-replacement program |
| Worried my girlfriend thinks she can't count on me | Talk to Lyndsey about 4-week plan |
| My industry may not exist ever again | Set up virtual meeting with career coach |
| I have no tenant | Post an ad for the condo at $2,400/month |
| Can't get a job | Apply to two jobs that interest you |

And there we had it. A to-do list of micro goals. Small but meaningful actions that would give Clint purpose over the next 4 weeks, actively making him feel safe because each action was combating a very real and deep-seated fear.

But as you know, in order to fully lift yourself out of panic mode, you need to be both safe *and* happy. These actions would make him feel safe, but I also wanted him to feel joy, to help give him hope again.

I made another list on the screen.

"Okay," I said, typing. "We're going to do the same thing, but for things that make you happy right now. Not happy forever, just over the next 4 weeks. I want you to think about what is making you happy *right now*."

He was silent for a moment. More than a moment. Too long really. We both burst out laughing.

"I know there's not a lot to be happy about right now," I said with a smile.

He smiled too. "No, but I see where you're going with this."

"Okay, so even if it's just one thing."

"Well, I'm really enjoying watching recorded live concerts of my favourite bands online. It's been a new thing that Lyndsey and I do remotely since lockdown started. We make snacks and watch concerts together, like a virtual date. Concerts we've been to together, some from bands in the 70s. It's fun. I don't think we would have ever done that otherwise."

I typed it in.

"What else?" I asked.

"I'm really enjoying not commuting."

"What does the extra time give you?"

"*Um,* sleep! I'm sleeping in until 7:30, 8:00 versus 5 a.m. Those two things are making me happy."

"Silver linings," I said. "Are there any times in the last week where you felt little to no anxiety?"

He thought. "On my walk to Lyndsey's place. Her room-mate is immune-compromised so we had a porch visit outside. It was snowing and so beautiful. With no cars on the road, it was pristine."

"Do you think that going for a walk or some access to nature could spark some joy?"

He laughed. "Yeah, for sure."

"Okay, so let's make some micro goals around those."

We went through the list line by line just as we had for his fears and filled in small, doable actions for the next 4 weeks.

| HAPPY | MICRO GOALS |
| --- | --- |
| Virtual concerts with Lyndsey | Two virtual concert dates |
| Sleeping in | Don't set alarm until 8 a.m. |
| Nature | Daily walk in the evening at 9 p.m. |

"How do you feel about these goals?" I asked.

"Good, actually. I love the idea of the nightly walk. That's when I'm the most anxious, especially because I'm alone. It's great for me to listen to a podcast or sometimes I'll try out a new band and listen to their album." He sighed. "I'm actually excited to do these."

"Why do you think that is?"

"I think I've been so focused on what I need to do to avoid disaster that I haven't really focused any energy on just taking care of myself or feeling happy for a moment. It feels good to know that simple things can still make me happy."

"Good," I said with a smile.

There it was. Safe and happy. I typed up his micro goals and emailed them over.

In the next 4 weeks (his micro timeline) Clint would:

1. Apply to government income-replacement programs.
2. Talk to Lyndsey about the micro timeline plan.
3. Set up a virtual meeting with a career coach.
4. Post an ad for the rental condo at $2,400/month.
5. Have two virtual concert dates.
6. Apply to two jobs that interest you.
7. Don't set an alarm before 8 a.m.
8. Take a daily evening walk.

He had full control over all of these small actions. They not only gave him purpose, they made him feel safe and happy at the same time, which stopped him from spiralling, even if just for a few weeks. That's the beauty of this activity. It's so simple but profound. By setting a micro timeline, he could actively choose activities and micro goals that promoted joy and alleviated anxiety.

Creating small, manageable goals and activities that make you feel joy within your micro timeline gives you a sense of moving forward without driving you to burnout.

Clint and I touched base every 4 weeks for several months. Once he had a new tenant and was breaking even financially every month, we graduated out of the micro space and back into the macro space. From short-term to long-term, to bigger decisions that needed to be made. Lyndsey did move into his apartment (a happy day indeed!), and they agreed that if the new tenant left and they couldn't find another within 4 weeks, they would move into the condo. Not forever, just for now. A damage control option.

He definitely did not want to sell the condo. Coming to that decision made all the other decisions easier.

As for schooling, he's still not sure what he's going to do, but he feels more optimistic that the travel industry will be able to pivot somehow, and he's hopeful that his employer will hire him back within the next 6 to 8 months. Because he's breaking even monthly now, he has less daily panic, so he can still wait to decide on his career without putting short-term safety at risk.

Because damage control in a crisis exists within a micro timeline, you can take slightly more extreme measures knowing it's only temporary. Very temporary. This isn't your life forever; it's just for now. There *is* an end date.

Micro timelines give you a sense of power over your life, even if the outcome isn't one you had planned on. In a crisis, damage can absolutely happen. Damage control lifts you out of panic mode because it gives you peace of mind that you're not spiralling, that you're not making things worse by delaying decisions on bigger issues.

You don't cancel the road trip because you have a flat tire.

You deal with the emergency in front of you and get back on highway when you can.

## HOMEWORK: CREATE MICRO TIMELINES

**Step 1:** Make a list of all the decisions you think you will have to make during your decision crisis.

**Step 2:** Choose a micro timeline. It's often helpful to align these with your pay periods from work. A micro timeline could also be as short as a week or as long as a month. If the crisis is a job loss and there is no pay period, then it's typically helpful to have a weekly micro timeline so that it gives you a sense of predictability and control. The shorter the timeline, the more predictable life feels and the less likely overwhelm can happen.

**Step 3:** List any short-term stakes where waiting longer than your micro timeline length would make you worse off than you are today. For example, if your micro timeline was

| DECISION(S) | EMERGENCY STAKES | LONG-TERM CORE VALUES/ GOAL |
| --- | --- | --- |
| Do I sell the condo? | Losing $2000/ month | Financial security, retirement income |

2 weeks, ask yourself, *What negative outcome will happen if I wait 2 weeks to make this decision?* Those are your emergency stakes. If nothing, put nothing. If something will happen—emotional stakes, financial stakes—put that into emergency stakes.

**Step 4:** List your core values for each decision. You can find this by asking yourself, *If I weren't in crisis, what would be important to me while making this decision?*

**Step 5:** Assess if waiting until the start of your next micro timeline will allow you to make a better choice. (This is a cost-benefit analysis.) Do you think reassessing in 2 weeks will give you an opportunity to get better information that will allow you to make a better decision than you could today?

**Step 6:** Create damage control options for any decision that has negative micro-timeline consequences of waiting and implement. See an example from Clint's story in the chart below.

| WILL WAITING GIVE YOU BETTER INFO? | DAMAGE CONTROL OPTION |
|---|---|
| Yes | Reduce expenses by $500, reduce rental price |

## HOMEWORK: CREATE MICRO GOALS

**Step 1:** List all the unknowns that are making you scared or anxious.

**Step 2:** List any micro goals (actions you can take within your micro timeline) that could help to appease this fear over the short run. What's one action you can do in the next 4 weeks to appease this fear? Here's an example from Clint's story to help you get started:

| SCARED/ANXIOUS | MICRO GOALS |
| --- | --- |
| My industry may not exist ever again | Set up virtual meeting with career coach |
|  |  |
|  |  |
|  |  |

**Step 3:** List anything happening in your life right now that is making you even remotely happy. Something that you are appreciative of or a silver lining.

**Step 4:** List any micro goals (actions you can take within your micro timeline) that could help to support this positive activity over the short run. What's one action you can do in the next 4 weeks to support an activity that will make you feel happier and less stressed?

| THINGS THAT MAKE ME HAPPY | MICRO GOALS |
|---|---|
| Sleeping in | Don't set alarm until 8 a.m. |
| | |
| | |
| | |

**Step 5:** Revisit and adjust at the end of each micro timeline.

Now you know how to pull yourself out of panic mode for the moment and hold on to that momentum. You know how to make yourself feel safe and happy. You know how to buy yourself time for important decisions without making things worse in the short run. And you know how to create a support network to help guide you through the next phase of your personal crisis. You can draw on these tools at any point in your crisis to make sure that you have a hopeful outlook when making big decisions.

With your outlook hopeful, it's time to start making decisions. The big ones. The ones that will impact the big picture. Your life. Your next normal. Who you will be on the other side of this crisis.

You're all set. Say goodbye to panic mode.

# PHASE 2:

## The Messy Middle

# CHAPTER 5:

## Getting to the Messy Middle

You've done a great job already. You've reached 60% normal, established a circle of care, and created micro timelines and goals that not only helped lift you out of panic mode for more than a moment but also bought you some time on big decisions without making things worse. You've done all of this in order to give yourself one very important thing: hope. A hopeful outlook is key when making big decisions. Without hope, you can't see that you have options or clearly identify what's truly important to you about the decision you're trying to make.

Without hope you lose the big picture. Everything feels uncertain and out of control, even when it isn't. Once you pull yourself out of panic mode, your options come into focus, and this is when reality hits. This is when it gets real and a hopeful outlook is needed most because this is the *messy middle.*

The messy middle is when you are no longer in panic mode all the time. You know there's no going back to life as you knew it, and you accept that you have to keep pushing forward toward your next normal. The grind of all the changes in your life are setting in, perhaps even stabilizing a bit. But things aren't over yet. You're still in it. It doesn't matter that you're tired, over it, or still surrounded by uncertainty. The time has come to actually make those big decisions. That's why the messy middle is often the hardest part. It's go time.

The worst part about a decision crisis is that you don't have a crystal ball. You can't see exactly how thing are going to play out. Maybe there's information overload. Maybe an information underload. Either way, you need to ensure you're ready to make a no-regret decision when the time comes.

I find that people often want to map out their potential options with hundreds of what-ifs. With so much confusion that comes during a crisis, overanalyzing can make sense, although overthinking can also make decisions more difficult. Things really could go a million different ways. It's not surprising people in panic mode approach decisions in polarized ways, either with an infinite number of what-if options or, conversely, black-and-white trade-off decisions.

Imagine a new parent who owns their own business, can't find childcare, and must return to work in 12 weeks.

What if I get a caregiver? What if I can't get a caregiver? What if I don't like the caregiver? What if I get a spot in a daycare centre after I hire the caregiver? What if I get a spot in the actual daycare that I want after I've accepted another place? What if I get the spot and can't afford the payments? What if I have to work part time? What if I can't pay for our life with part-time work? What if I brought the baby with me to work?

Imagine that all of your options were mapped out like a tree—a decision tree. With each branch representing a potential what-if outcome. It would look like a spiral graph if you mapped out all potential outcomes with all the what-ifs out of your control. This part of the book is like decision tree bonsai, where we ensure you're not making trade-off decisions in panic mode or drowning in what-if options. Systematically paring down your choices will leave you with what's most important to you, give you some predictability in the short run, and ensure you don't go off the rails. In this part of the Decision Crisis Playbook, you will create a plan of attack for the series of difficult decisions you need to make so you don't regret those decisions later on.

In the messy middle, you need to:

1. Figure out your deciding values.
2. Assign any short-term predictability where you can.
3. Learn when you need to pivot your plans.
4. Create boundaries (guardrails) for yourself so that you don't waste time or money as you decide.

These crucial steps will help you generate options and pull the trigger on your decision(s) to ensure you are proud of your choices even if things don't pan out the way you planned. You'll have confidence that you made the best decision you could at the time.

# CHAPTER 6:

## Determining Your

## Deciding Values

By now you're probably breathing easier, knowing you've taken all the right steps to lead you here, where you'll master the techniques necessary to discover your own core values. You already know that a huge part of being at peace with your next normal is actually enjoying your day-to-day life on the other side of your decision crisis. It may sound obvious, but the best possible decisions you can make are ones that uphold your core values the best way they can. Your core values are a set of beliefs that are important to you and you alone. They determine what you prioritize in your life and, ultimately, whether or not your life is the one you want to be living. If you're living a daily life that aligns with your core values, you're satisfied, content, and at peace. Life feels fulfilling. If you're living a daily life where your core values are violated, you feel frustrated, unsatisfied, and even resentful. Assessing your core values is crucial when it comes to big life decisions.

The typical way to find out about someone's values is to have them to envision when they are happiest. Who is there? What are they doing?

I'll typically ask questions like *What need is being fulfilled? What is your best-case scenario?* or *How would this give meaning to your life?*

Then, we go through a list of core values (like the one on pages 112–13), identify which resonate for the client, and prioritize them. I do this exercise with clients all the time.

I always ask clients to re-establish their core values when they are in a decision crisis, even if they've been my client for years. Why? Because our values change as we change. When I was younger, *vision* and *usefulness* were probably my top priorities. At this moment in my life, *family* and *positivity* have taken top spots. That doesn't mean *vision* and *usefulness* aren't there, but they've taken a slight back seat in the family minivan. So when I'm making big decisions today, I'll prioritize my family life and self-care over my career ambitions in a way I simply could not have imagined when I was 25. Admitting this hurts a bit. Even writing that down makes my 25-year-old, ambitious-AF self cringe. But this will likely change again one day. Who knows? Another 15 years from now my core values may change back or change in another way I can't yet imagine. Every decision we make has a different core value based on where we are in life—they aren't set in stone forever.

The way you prioritize your core values can, and likely will, change if you're in a crisis situation or major life transition. Things that may have been a top priority pre-crisis may now have shifted to another spot or maybe they don't even matter anymore.

When someone is in the messy middle of their decision crisis, I like to tap into something I call your *deciding values*. Of all of your core values (there are probably many), your deciding values are the most important in the moment. These are the values that you're going to prioritize at this specific time in your life in order to make a decision you won't regret.

The best way to flush out your values when you're making big decisions is to map out your best- and worst-case scenarios. In your best-case scenario, your deciding values are usually the ones you're most afraid of violating in your worst-case scenario. If you think about that, it makes sense. When the things that are most important to you don't work out, the situation becomes your worst-case scenario. So by laying out the best and worst cases, and then scanning for the common core values, your deciding values become clear, and a huge overwhelming decision tree with seemingly endless branches is quickly narrowed down to a few key decisions.

## CORE VALUES

| | | | |
|---|---|---|---|
| Accountability | Cheerfulness | Courtesy | Effectiveness | Family |
| Accuracy | Clear-mindedness | Creativity | Efficiency | Fidelity |
| Achievement | Commitment | Curiosity | Elegance | Fitness |
| Adventurousness | Community | Decisiveness | Empathy | Fluency |
| Altruism | Compassion | Democraticness | Enjoyment | Focus |
| Ambition | Competitiveness | Dependability | Enthusiasm | Freedom |
| Assertiveness | Consistency | Determination | Equality | Fun |
| Balance | Contentment | Devoutness | Excellence | Generosity |
| Being the best | Continuous | Diligence | Excitement | Goodness |
| Belonging | improvement | Discipline | Expertise | Grace |
| Boldness | Contribution | Discretion | Exploration | Growth |
| Calmness | Control | Diversity | Expressiveness | Happiness |
| Carefulness | Cooperation | Dynamism | Fairness | Hard work |
| Challenge | Correctness | Economy | Faith | Health |

Helping society
Holiness
Honesty
Honour
Humility
Independence
Ingenuity
Inner harmony
Inquisitiveness
Insightfulness
Intelligence
Intellectual status
Intuition
Joy
Justice
Leadership
Legacy
Love

Loyalty
Making a difference
Mastery
Merit
Obedience
Openness
Order
Originality
Patriotism
Perfection
Piety
Positivity
Practicality
Preparedness
Professionalism
Prudence
Quality

Reliability
Resourcefulness
Restraint
Results-oriented
Rigor
Financial security
Self-actualization
Self-control
Selflessness
Self-reliance
Sensitivity
Serenity
Service
Shrewdness
Simplicity
Soundness
Speed
Spontaneity

Stability
Strategic
Strength
Structure
Success
Support
Teamwork
Temperance
Thankfulness
Thoroughness
Thoughtfulness
Timeliness
Tolerance
Traditionalism
Trustworthiness
Truth-seeking
Understanding
Uniqueness

Unity
Usefulness
Vision
Vitality

## MEET YASMIN

AGE: 42

RELATIONSHIP STATUS: Going through a messy
separation/divorce

KIDS: 2 (ages 7 and 10)

Email sent at 2 a.m. reads:

> *Hey Shannon,*
>
> *Sunil and I have separated. I am so anxious about all the big changes ahead. For the past 6 months I've been renting (way over budget, I think, anyways) and dipping into what I will be owed from the buyout of the matrimonial home. Gah! I'll be getting about $300,000 from sale of our house, no spousal support, and $3,000 a year in child support. I'm freaking out. Help.*

Response:

> *Let's get you in for a meeting ASAP.*

I met with Yasmin several times throughout her separation and eventual divorce. Yasmin had been married for 15 years. She had recently taken a stress leave from work because the heartbreak of divorce and the stress of uncertainty, and the intense financial and emotional stakes were crippling her emotionally, physically, and psychologically. She was in the midst of a personal crisis.

"Big changes ahead," I said during our first meeting.

"You're telling me." She was smiling but her jaw was tight and her back very straight. Too straight.

"How are you feeling about the changes?" I prodded.

She shook her head. "I have no f*cking idea."

I nodded. "Divorce is so hard. Even the most amicable ones."

She took a sharp breath and nodded quickly without looking up. It was clear she was on the verge of tears or already crying. She kept her head down, and we sat in silence until she felt ready to speak again.

"So much is unknown, you know?" she said, her voice cracking slightly. "And it sucks."

"Tell me what sucks about it."

"My poor kids. I don't want them going through this. Seeing me like this, seeing Sunil like this. Moving around and not sure if they can stay at their school with their friends. I hate the uncertainty it has created for them. I feel so guilty."

I nodded, even though I knew she didn't have anything to feel guilty about. But the whole "kids are resilient" and "this isn't your fault" affirmations would have been inappropriate in the moment. She was hurting and sad, and it felt like she just wanted to be honest without having me push a "stay positive" message.

"What's your worst-case scenario here?" I asked.

"Worst case?" She raised her eyebrows.

"Worst case," I said.

"Oh, god." She paused. "*Ha,* I don't even like thinking about it."

"Well, we're gonna."

She let out a sigh. "Okay, worst case is that $3,000 in child support doesn't help with any of the future costs for the kids. That I can't actually afford to buy a home in our school district so I'll have to move somewhere else and might have to rent. My kids will have to change schools, and I'll have a much longer commute so I'll hate my life, see them much less, and they won't be able to make it to their extracurriculars because I'll get home too late. Basically, their entire world will be upside down because I don't make enough money to sustain our current life by myself."

I was listening to what values were coming up. Using someone's worst-case scenario is often viewed as wallowing in panic, closing off options, cementing those trade-off, scarcity mindsets. To a degree, that's true, but over the years I've learned that letting someone really flush out their worst-case scenario in the midst of a decision crisis can be the key to uncovering not only their core values but the true priority of them. This gives us their deciding values.

"Tell me what's at stake if your worst-case scenario plays out?"

"My sanity," she said and took a long swig of tea.

We both laughed.

"What do you mean by 'my sanity'?"

She shifted uncomfortably in the very comfortable chair.

"I will be heartbroken for the kids if they have to change schools or can't make it to their extracurriculars. And I'd hate to see so much less of them."

"This is what I'm hearing if your worst case plays out," I said and showed her the list I'd been making while she talked.

## WORST-CASE SCENARIO STAKES:

- Kids change schools
- Long commute (personal happiness)
- Kids have no extracurriculars
- Have to rent (versus buy) a home

She looked over the list, nodding. "Yep, that about sums it up."

"Now," I said, "what's your best-case scenario?"

*"Hmmm."* She looked up at the ceiling. "I can actually afford to buy a place. I can stay in the school area so the kids and I still have friends. I don't have to commute and the kids stay in their school. Basically, there's little disruption in our lives, but I'm not willing to set myself up for financial ruin to do so."

I was furiously taking notes. "Okay, so the best-case scenario stakes are as follows."

## BEST-CASE SCENARIO STAKES:

- Kids stay in same school
- No long commute
- Kids remain in their usual extracurriculars
- You keep your community
- You can purchase a home you can afford

She read over the list.

"Yep. That's it, right there."

I put the lists side by side.

| WORST-CASE SCENARIO STAKES | BEST-CASE SCENARIO STAKES |
|---|---|
| • Kids change schools<br>• Long commute (personal happiness)<br>• Kids have no extracurriculars<br>• Have to rent (versus buy) a home | • Kids stay in same school<br>• No long commute<br>• Kids remain in their usual extracurriculars<br>• You keep your community<br>• You can purchase a home you can afford |

"Let's drill down a bit. In your worst-case scenario, what is important to you about your kids staying in their current school?"

"They keep their community of friends and their teachers. My kids are both thriving right now."

"What value do you think would be violated if they had to change schools?"

She thought about it for some time. "I don't really know how to put it into words."

"Have a read through these." I handed her the list of core values. "Any of those feel like the right word?"

She took her time with it.

"Actually, I think *joy* is the right word."

"How so?"

"Seeing my kids thrive at their school gives me joy. Without some joy, what's the point of anything?"

"So having joy in your life is not merely important, it's vital, making it a core value. Making sure the kids thrive will uphold that value."

"Yes."

"And you'd be violating that if the kids weren't thriving?"

She nodded in agreement.

"Great. What about the kids in extracurriculars? What's important to you about that?"

"The same thing. It's them thriving."

"So the way to honour your core value of joy is to do whatever you can to ensure the kids thrive in their new life."

"Yes."

I moved to the next line in the worst-case scenario list.

"What about the commute? What's at stake if you have to commute?"

"I worry that in order to afford to buy something, I'll have to move far away, which will mean driving to work or taking transit. "

"And if that happens?"

"I won't get to pick them up from school, and I love doing that so much. I know that people all over the world commute every day and their kids are thriving. I'm not worried about them thriving if I can't pick them up."

"Then what are you worried about?" I asked.

"Well, for me, the walk home is where I get the best info on how their day actually was. By dinner, it's a shrug and 'It was fine.' Plus, I hate commuting."

"So what values would be violated if you commuted?"

She consulted the list again and laughed. "Time with family, time together after school. I want to feel like I know my kids."

"So the values being violated in your worst-case scenario are joy and family time, both of which will be upheld as long as you feel the kids are thriving and you get quality time with them."

"Exactly."

"Okay, let's look at the best-case scenario."

| WORST-CASE SCENARIO STAKES | BEST-CASE SCENARIO STAKES |
| --- | --- |
| • Kids change schools<br>• Long commute (personal happiness)<br>• Kids have no extracurriculars<br>• Have to rent (versus buy) a home | • Kids stay in same school<br>• No long commute<br>• Kids remain in their usual extracurriculars<br>• You keep your community<br>• You can purchase a home you can afford |

"What values are being *honoured* if you buy a home you can afford in a neighbourhood that lets the kids stay in their current school with their existing extracurriculars, and you don't have a long commute?"

She gave me a knowing look and a smile. "The kids are still thriving and I get to hang out with them more frequently."

I smiled back.

"So joy and family," she said. "It's the same."

"It *is* the same. Most times, the core values being violated in our worst-case scenario reflect the core values being upheld in our best-case scenario. That's how we know they are something I call *deciding values,* which are the values that we use to guide your decisions."

"So joy and family are my deciding values?"

"They are. But I also see one more core value here."

She looked at the list and then back to me with a furrowed brow.

I motioned to the best-case scenario list. "In your best-case scenario, you've purchased a home, and as you've said many times, it's a home you can afford. In your worst-case scenario, you've said two things that conflict about home purchase."

"What do you mean?"

"Well, in your best-case scenario, you mention affordability. What core value do you think is being upheld if you purchase a home you can afford?"

She didn't need to look at the list. "Financial security. Not being destitute in retirement or house poor."

"But in your worst-case scenario, you not only list having to pay rent but also include having to move far away to find something you can afford to buy, which would mean pulling the kids out of school. So between renting here or buying farther away, which is the worst case for you?

"I didn't think about that."

I sat back, giving her time to mull it over.

"I think," she said after a few minutes, "that the actual worst case is renting something farther away."

"Why is that worse than renting something close?"

"Because if I rented close, I would assume the kids can stay in their school. So I'm upholding that value of family time with no commute, and joy because the kids will have the least disruption. If I rent far away, none those values will be upheld, plus I won't have the financial security of being mortgage-free one day."

I nodded. "So financial security is important, but it's not really about renting versus owning."

"Right. It's more about making sure I'm not being bad with money."

"Okay. So from all this, we can clearly see your three deciding values."

1. Kids thriving
2. Family time
3. Financial security

"Are those typical?" she asked.

"There are no typical core values for people. What's important to each person is so different. What you think is good varies wildly from what others think is good. Neither is right or wrong. Just different."

She nodded. "Okay, so now that we have this, how does it help me decide between a condo or a townhouse? Or whether to stay where we are or venture farther out?"

"To begin, this isn't a decision about apartment versus condo versus townhouse. This is about making a decision that will help you feel like you've made the best choice to help your kids thrive while maintaining quality time with them and financial security."

She sat with that for a moment then said, "Seeing it this way feels so obvious and oversimplified."

"It is, in a way. But once the hard decisions are made, everything else is just details and logistics, neither of which factor into the actual decision. What's important is knowing you made your choice with these values in mind. If you do, the chances of regret later are so much less. It won't matter if it's a house, condo, apartment, or even where you live or if you rent or own as long as you feel like the kids are thriving, you have time with them, and enough wiggle room to retire one day."

"That's so true." She paused for a moment. "But what if I genuinely can't afford those things?"

"What I'm hearing in that question is *What happens if my value of financial security conflicts with my values of joy and family time?*"

She grinned and rolled her eyes at me. "Sure. Okay. Yes."

I laughed. "To answer that question, we need to prioritize your deciding values." I started another list.

1. Would you rather be house poor (jeopardizing financial security) but feel like you set your kids up the best you could for them to thrive (ensuring joy)?

"Kids thrive," she said, matter-of-factly.

2. Would you rather have your kids stay in their current school (kids thrive) or be able to walk home with them (family time)?

"School," she said.

3. Would you rather be house poor (again, jeopardizing financial security) but have your walk home with them (again, ensuring family time)?

"Family time," she said.

"So now we know that setting up your kids for the best chance to thrive is your number-one priority, which upholds your need to honour joy in your life. We also know that family time trumps financial security, but that financial security is still important."

"It is. I don't think my kids will thrive if I put them into a situation where I'm always stressed."

"Exactly. I think there's a point where you'll rob yourself of joy if you feel financially insecure."

"Totally."

"What could happen that would make you put financial security above keeping your kids in their current school?"

She stared at the desk a moment then raised her head. "I'd have to be going into serious debt, so much so that I couldn't afford their extracurriculars. If we could never take a family vacation, I'd be stressed."

"What core value would be violated if that happened?"

"Kids thriving," she said again, laughing.

"I agree. So financial security is not your top priority unless it threatens your joy or the ability to set up your kids to thrive."

She nodded.

"Great." I smiled. "Now we know."

"Now we know what?"

"Now we know how to tackle any decision throughout your divorce so that you will be confident in your choice later on, no matter how the details get worked out. Your deciding values—family time, having joy in your life, and financial security—are your North Star, so to speak. All the other stuff you're worrying about are just details and logistics. Your deciding values are what's at stake. Keeping them top of mind will help you make all the difficult decisions in front of you."

"I never thought about it like this."

"When we come down to it, your decisions have to centre around this question: *How do I make sure I set up my kids for their best shot at thriving, have enough family time to feel like I know them, and ensure that I won't be house poor or destitute in retirement?*"

She didn't say anything right away. Then, after about a minute, she said, "It seems so much clearer now."

I smiled. "That's because it is."

For Yasmin, we knew that her deciding values were, in order of importance: setting kids up to thrive (joy), feeling like she knew her kids (family), and financial security. Now she needed to decide what to do with the $300,000 payout she got from the sale of the matrimonial home.

When she initially sat down with me, she was trying to decide whether she should live in a townhouse versus a condo, whether she should rent versus own; what neighbourhood they should live in, whether she could keep the kids at their school along with their extracurriculars, how to maintain her RRSP contributions, how to avoid being house poor—the list went on and on. But after figuring out her deciding values, we were able to quiet the noise and focus on the fact that no matter what decision she made, she could sleep knowing she had done everything possible to help her kids continue to thrive, maintain her family time, and have enough financial security so that she wasn't stressed all the time, which would rob her of joy.

"There are really only three options now," I pointed out.

"Versus a million," she said.

We wrote them out.

**Option 1:** Buy a home in the neighbourhood. Use 100% of the $300,000 as a down payment. She would no longer be able to afford extracurricular activities for the kids, but they would stay in their school. Yasmin would have no worries about her housing and there would be no commuting. On the downside, she would not be able to save for retirement.

**Option 2:** Rent in the neighbourhood, put the $300,000 toward retirement. The kids would stay in their school and Yasmin would be able to afford extracurricular activities. In addition, she would not have to commit to a mortgage and could achieve some financial security. But she would still have worries about housing displacement if she were to be evicted.

**Option 3:** Move father away and buy a less expensive home. Use 100% of the $300,000 for a down payment. She could still afford extracurricular activities and keep her long-term retirement security on track by paying a lower mortgage. On the downside, her commute would be longer, and her kids would have to start at a new school.

"So I get that these uphold my values, but aren't I financially screwed with Option 1?" she said.

"Not necessarily, although the long-term retirement security piece is under threat. In Option 1, you have the ability to be mortgage-free one day, but you'll have no ability to save between now and then. So come retirement, you'll have to move, to downsize, unless in the short-term your income went up drastically."

"Or I'd have to win the lottery," she said dryly.

I laughed. "Or that."

"Option 2 is interesting," I said. "The kids would stay in the school they love, you'd have family time and the ability to save some money for retirement, but you wouldn't have secure housing or equity in a property of your own."

She put her hands to her face and covered her eyes. "So I have to move. That's what you're saying."

I smiled mischievously. "No, I'm saying you need to make a values-based decision." I pointed to her deciding values list. "What exactly does 'kids thriving' mean to you?"

She let out a fake exasperated breath. "It means that they are happy."

"Okay, so let's say that Option 3 plays out and you move. They have to go to a different school and leave their current community, and you'd have to commute, but you're financially secure."

The expression on her face indicated that she did not like this option.

"Just hear me out," I said. "What deciding values are you upholding here in this option?"

"The financial security one," she said.

"Are you sure that's it?"

"Yes. If they have to leave their school and communities, and I have to commute, the final decision is all about the finances."

"What happens if they leave their school?"

"They have to make new friends. And we'll only get to see our old community on weekends and at extracurriculars."

"And you're worried that means they won't thrive."

"Yes."

"Okay, what about Option 1: Buy a home in the neighbourhood? Use 100% of the $300,000 down payment. Not be able to afford extracurriculars for the kids, but they stay in their school. No worries about being displaced for housing.

No commute. But long-term retirement security is threatened," I read. "Are the kids thriving here?"

"Yes." She hesitated. "Well, I hope they will be thriving."

"What do you mean?" I asked.

"Well, it's great that they can stay at their school. But if they can't participate in their extracurricular activities because I can't afford them, then I'll probably be stressed and they won't be happy either in the long run. But who knows what life will look like 5 years from now?"

"What is stressful about Option 1 to you?"

"The money. In the short term, I know I'd be house poor. My neighbourhood has become too expensive."

"What about the long run?"

"I'm not sure. Maybe less? I could get another job, I could get big raises, that lottery ticket."

"I agree. With Option 1, you're upholding your deciding value around family time. The kids thriving is unpredictable, especially over the longer run, and all of this at the cost of your other deciding value of long-term financial security.

"What's different about Option 2?"

"Well," she said. "The kids' thriving thing is the same. If I rent in the neighbourhood, I'm not house poor. The big difference is that I can save money if I rent and the kids can still attend their extracurricular activities."

"But . . ."

"But what if I got evicted? What if I can't find a place to live after that or can't afford to buy a home then? There are a lot of unknowns there too. So, again, the core value around financial security is sort of violated."

"Lots of life to unfold." I looked down at the list. "What about Option 3? Do you know for a fact that the kids would be unhappy and that they won't thrive if they change schools?"

She looked me right in the eyes. "No," she said and raised an eyebrow.

"Go on." I smiled.

"Moving would be really hard on them."

I didn't say anything.

She sighed. "I know, you're right. They could make new friends, thrive there. I know, I know."

She put her hands up, like a surrender. I giggled.

"You just had a whole conversation with yourself. So what makes Option 3 so unappealing to you? It's upholding your deciding value of financial security for sure, and it is possible it eventually upholds your deciding value of your kids' thriving."

"Two things: First, I don't want them to be disrupted at this point in their schooling. Second, I want some personal pleasure too. I feel like the commute thing is a huge issue and guaranteed to eat into that family time in the short run. Over the long run, they will grow up and the pickup time won't matter as much 5 years from now. It's really just a short-term problem."

"So how do you feel about the options now?"

"I'm actually surprised I'm going to say this, but buying in my neighbourhood feels like the worst choice, even though it's what I want to do the most."

"Why is that?"

"I think the idea of being house poor, not being able to afford extracurriculars, and putting financial security on the line is scarier than the idea of them starting over at a new school. It's possible they would thrive, but there's not a lot of hope for my finances if I buy here."

"What about Option 2?"

"I think I need to sit with that. The worry about being disrupted again if the landlord decides they don't want to rent anymore. The idea of going through this all over again is scary. I also realize that I'm sitting here making all these decisions for my kids without actually talking to them about what they need to be happy."

"Why do you think you avoided that thought before?" I asked.

"I don't think I really knew what the options or the choices were. I couldn't articulate them, and I didn't want to scare them. But now I feel like I can have a really direct conversation with them and see which option they love most, which will uphold my deciding value of helping them thrive."

"I couldn't agree more. You need to think about which option would leave you with the least amount of regret should the worst-case scenario come to pass."

Yasmin left my office with her options laid out, knowing which ones upheld her values versus the ones that did not or that were completely out of her control.

She hadn't made a choice yet, but she knew what those no-regret decisions were.

About 2 weeks later, I got a call from Yasmin.

"So?" I asked, anxiously.

"We are going to rent in the neighbourhood. Option 2."

"Okay, great!" I noted that she used the word *we*, meaning she had brought her kids into the conversation.

"What tipped it over the edge for you?"

"I realized that Option 2 not only gave us the best chance at happiness all around, it also reinforced that their thriving is my highest priority when it comes to decision-making. Above family time and above my financial security. For better or worse. My kids are only in school for another 10 years until post-secondary. I can re-evaluate then depending on my career, their lives, my non-existent lottery winnings. And if I want to use the money from the sale of the house to buy something then, I still can."

"What about the risk of eviction?"

"My kids didn't care about it. They would rather risk it now while they still go to school here, and we'll deal with it—if we have to—down the road."

"How do you feel?"

"I feel the same way now! Something about bringing them into the conversation alleviated some of the guilt if the plan goes awry. We all chose this option together and have some faith that we will make it through the next 10 years."

"So even if the worst-case scenario plays out and you have to move in less than 5 years, will you still feel empowered that Option 2 is the best choice you can make right now?"

"Totally. Anything else feels like I'm setting myself up for failure. Financial or emotional. Either way, it's not enough."

"You sound settled."

"I am. I really don't believe I'm going to be ruining my life or theirs anymore."

"Good," I said with a smile.

A few months later, Yasmin and I sat down for another check-in. She had rented a townhouse in her neighbourhood. The rent was in line with what she could afford and would still allow her to save a bit for retirement while still being able to afford the extracurriculars her kids enjoyed without slipping into debt.

She had upheld her most important deciding values. By laying out Yasmin's best- and worst-case scenarios, we were able to take a huge problem with so many potential decisions to worry about and boil it down to three specific deciding values. By prioritizing them, she was able to confidently decide on an option that upheld all three at once but especially honoured her most important deciding value: the kids' thriving. Sometimes this is why people get stuck in analysis paralysis. There are too many potential outcomes. Without deciphering what the priority of your deciding values are, all potential outcomes seem equally important, when they aren't.

Deciding values will help you stay focused on what actually matters to you and will guide you through your decision crisis.

## HOMEWORK: FIND YOUR DECIDING VALUES

**Step 1:** Write out your worst-case scenario.

**Step 2:** Consult the list of core values. Write down as many core values as you can for this worst-case scenario. What values would be violated if this worst-case situation played out?

**Step 3:** Write out your best-case scenario.

**Step 4:** Consult the list of core values. Write down as many core values as you can for this best-case scenario. What values would you be honouring if this best-case situation played out?

**Step 5:** Circle the similar ones. Aim for 1 to 3. These are your deciding values.

**Step 6:** Prioritize your top three.

# CHAPTER 7:

## Assigning Decision Predictability

Once you've got your deciding values figured out, the next task is to assess your options and choose any that offer some degree of predictability. While deciding values are the key to finding peace of mind and being proud of your choices later on, *decision predictability* is vital to letting go of, or acknowledging, outcomes you can't control and often choosing an option that offers some short-term predictability.

Decision predictability allows you to generate actionable and realistic options that will give you some—or at least the illusion of—control. Of course, nothing is 100% predictable. Life would be so boring if it were. But I think that in the short term, we do have a small level of predictability or control.

Making decisions with some degree of short-term predictability is a great way to prioritize your options before making big decisions with high stakes so you'll always know you made the best decision with the information you had at the time.

I often hear clients say, *If someone could just guarantee that X would happen, then I'd know what to do,* and to be honest, I've said it myself when I have to make tough choices.

But that's not our reality at all. If you could control the outcome, you wouldn't be in a decision crisis. The truth is, we don't control much in life. I know it, you know it. That's why they call them "gut feelings," not "gut guarantees." That's not to say that I don't believe in intuition or hunches. Quite the opposite. But over the years, I've learned that our gut instincts, or hunches, or whatever you want to call them, usually come from feelings around our deciding values versus our ability to control outcomes or predict the future.

Assigning short-term predictability to your options is the only way to let go of outcomes that are beyond your control. Like the weather.

Let's use the weather as an example. Say you're planning an important picnic. A big deal, everyone-is-coming community picnic. You received a small grant from the town to help with the expenses, and the entire event is your responsibility. You've been working on decorations for the trees, you sewed a picnic blanket, and you made all the food in order to stay within the grant budget. A week before the picnic, the weather network is calling for a 50% chance of thunderstorms. What do you do?

Let's say your deciding values are bring the community together (*community* being the value), being prepared (*preparedness* as a value), and helping others (*kindness*). What are your options for the picnic when there's a 50/50 chance of a thunderstorm?

### Option 1: YOLO (You Only Live Once)

Do nothing. Roll with it. Go for it and hope it works out. Best-case scenario: It doesn't rain.

### Option 2: Reschedule

The risk here is that next week, fewer people may be able to come because you've moved the date and the weather could still be an issue. Best-case scenario: Everyone comes and it's a perfectly sunny day.

### Option 3: Covered pavilion

Imagine there was a covered pavilion in the park, available for private events. It costs $500 to rent for the day, giving you a Plan B in case it rains. Best-case scenario: You have a backup plan in place—but it's still risky because you have reached the maximum on the grant budget. That $500 would be paid out of your pocket, and you can't guarantee everyone will come if there is a thunderstorm.

Let's examine each option and assign predictability on a scale of 0 to 5 in the short run versus long run: 0 being as random as the weather two months from now and 5 meaning 100% guaranteed.

**Option 1: YOLO**
Does Option 1 provide any short-term predictability?
No. You're 100% dependent on the weather. 0/5

Does Option 1 provide any long-term predictability?
No, you're 100% dependent on the weather. 0/5

That doesn't mean you don't or can't choose Option 1; it just means you're acknowledging that you're taking a flyer here. There's zero control or predictability in the short or long run, but you don't care. You have faith it will all work out. If it doesn't, at least you know you tried your best and went into it with your eyes wide open. That's how you have zero regrets on the other end. You upheld your deciding values so that even though it doesn't work out, you are still proud of your choice. In your opinion, which is all that matters, you made the right decision *for you* at the time.

**Option 2: Reschedule**
Does Option 2 provide any short-term predictability?
Yes. You can reschedule so that the weather on the date of the original picnic doesn't affect you anymore. You have full control over cancelling the

event. Cancelling the picnic guarantees you'll have no weather risk this Sunday. 5/5.

Does Option 2 provide any long-term predictability? No, you're 100% dependent on the weather again, plus people may not be able to attend now. 0/5.

You can choose Option 2 but trying to predict or control future weather is not possible so you'll still be facing the YOLO situation, except now you risk having fewer people in attendance.

## Option 3: Covered pavilion for $500

Does Option 3 provide any short-term predictability? Yes. If you can afford it, you can rent it for your event, just in case. 5/5

Does Option 3 provide any long-term predictability? Yes. The weather on Sunday matters but not as much because you have some coverage. So it's not 5/5 because it may still be cold, the wind may be high, but you can shelter yourself from the brunt of the randomness of the weather. 3/5

What do you choose?

If I said you could safely afford to pay $500, you'd probably choose Option 3. If I told you that $500 would sink you financially, you probably wouldn't. But what if you knew that Option 3 was the best decision as long as it was afford-able? If you came up with an idea for everyone in the community to donate $10 to rent it, you might go ahead with that choice. Keeping the values and goals in mind, I'd say this is the best option (but only if the money can be raised quickly).

The point is, generating options and choosing the ones that have some degree of short-term predictability is usually the best call. This is how you assign decision predictability. It gives you a sense of control and ensures that you've made the best possible choices you could at the time given the information at hand.

## MEET ANIKA
AGE: 37
RELATIONSHIP STATUS: Single
CHILDREN: None

Two months ago, Anika invested $10,000 into her retirement account for the first time. It was her first experience with investing. She told me, at the time, that she had been sitting on the cash for over a year, too afraid to make the jump from a safe savings account earning less than 1% a month to investing. She had endlessly researched, read blogs, books, listened to podcasts, but when push came to shove, she was too scared. She finally took the plunge and, less than 2 months later during the first wave of COVID-19, her portfolio was down from $10,000 to $7,800. A 22% drop. That's a big drop. A terrifying one. Even for a seasoned investor.

"I want to cash it out," she said the moment her face appeared on my computer screen. Her eyes were wide, and she had a no-bullshit look on her face.

During our previous in-person financial meeting 3 months earlier, Anika told me that the $10,000 was her nest egg. It was earmarked for retirement. She had a long time horizon and a high risk tolerance. I had been very clear that investing comes with ups and downs. Stock and bond markets have volatility. That's normal. I remember telling her, "Everyone has a high investment risk tolerance (meaning they are okay with their money potentially going down by a lot in exchange for bigger potential for it to go up) until their money goes down. Recessions, market corrections, and bear markets are where you really find out what your true risk tolerance is."

Little did we know that her personal lesson would start almost instantly.

"Okay, take a deep breath," I said.

I think it's important to note that I don't make money from client investments. I'm an advice-only financial planner and my company does not sell any investment products. Whether she invested or cashed out had no impact on my income or our company revenue whatsoever. My only goal was to make sure she was making the best choices for her long-term financial goals and would not have regrets later on.

"Tell me what's happening," I said.

"Pretty obvious, isn't it? I've lost over 20% of my money in a matter of weeks."

"How would cashing out now help you?"

"I'd stop losing money," she said flatly.

"That's true. But you'd also be locking in that loss."

"What do you mean?"

"What you're seeing on your screen is just what your investments are worth today if you cash them out. They could be up tomorrow or down by more. The goal and the hope with investing is that you buy low and sell high over time, right? Selling now would mean that you bought high and sold low. Once you cash it in, that's that. There's no earning the money back. Does that make sense?"

"Yes, but what if it keeps going down?"

"That's totally possible," I said. "No one can see the future, and anyone who says they can is trying to sell you something."

She grimaced.

"Let's start by recalling what this money means to you before you decide what to do. Then we'll work on making the best possible decision. When we last met, this money was the start of your retirement nest egg. Is that still true?"

"Yes."

"So what's at stake if this keeps dropping below the amount it is today?"

"I'm 37. I'm single and that's all I have saved after taking a decade to pay off my student loan. I have $10,000—or *had* $10,000—to my name for retirement."

"What's your best-case scenario here?" I asked.

"Essentially what we planned before: Invest the money, make my money grow over time. Maybe a 4 to 5% rate of return, on average, over time."

I was proud of her for having such realistic expectations for her best-case scenario.

"And what happens if the current $7,800 drops lower, say to $6,000?"

She raised an eyebrow, looking at me like I was just a little dense and missing the obvious. "It makes it harder for me to have financial security down the road."

I knew she was getting a bit frustrated, and I wasn't trying to downplay her anxiety. But if I've learned anything about good decision-making, it's that the stakes really need to be flushed out. "So your deciding value here is long-term financial security," I said.

She nodded. "It has to be. I'm alone. It's all up to me."

At last, we were getting to the heart of her fear, uncovering what mattered most to her.

"How would locking in this $2,200 ($10,000 – $7,800) loss help to honour your deciding value of long-term financial security?"

"It would mean I didn't lose any more. At least I could control the outcome."

"That's true," I said. "And what else?"

She sighed and looked down at her desk. "It also means I'd probably earn like 1% and there would no growth opportunity."

"What's your worst-case scenario here?" I asked.

"It goes to zero and never recovers."

"What scares you about that?" I asked.

"I'd have to start over."

"Let's say your worst-case scenario plays out," I said. "If the $10,000 did go to zero, do you think long-term retirement security is totally off the table for you?"

She thought about that. "No, I guess not. I still have 30 years to save, but I worry about the $250 a month that I have automatically going into the account. I don't want that to go to zero as well, and I don't want to feel like an idiot or that I made the wrong decision."

"You're not an idiot at all. What makes you feel like that?"

She let out long breath. "I don't know," she said and shrugged. "That somehow I've been taken advantage of or been had. Or that I missed something. It sounds paranoid."

"Not paranoid. It sounds like you're afraid. Which means your worst-case scenario isn't just about losing $10,000. It's about not regretting your financial decisions."

"Yes. I think you're right. It's maybe not regret. More like failure. When things don't work out, or things fail, I take it very personally. Like, I truly believe that I should have seen this coming and, because I didn't, I can't trust myself to make good decisions. No matter how much research I did, I took the risk anyways, and now that it's plummeting in value, maybe I shouldn't have."

"How do you usually make sure you don't have regrets?"

"Well, usually, in other circumstances, I try to do my due diligence. I make sure that I've done enough research to ensure I make right decision."

"You arm yourself with knowledge."

"Yes. I use information to try to minimize risk and control the outcome."

I thought about this.

"Control is interesting in the context of investing," I said.

"You're telling me," she said, and it was the first time she smiled the entire time.

I smiled, knowingly. "So I don't have to tell you that you have no real control when it comes to investment market performance."

She laughed. "I know."

"So then, how did you get to a place in February where you were able to relinquish control and invest proudly? What was different then, from now?"

"I had been sitting with that $10,000 in a savings account for over a year. It earned like $100 the whole year. At first, I was okay with that. I thought, *It's earning less than 1%, but at least I know what it's going to be,* and it didn't feel stupid to me because I hadn't learned anything about investing. I didn't have the knowledge, but I had control. So it was okay."

"What changed?"

"I started to feel stupid for having the money in an account that had less than 1% interest. I am debt free, I've got emergency savings, and this money is earmarked for retirement. Keeping it in a savings account wasn't even keeping pace with inflation. Once I had done all this research, I knew it would help my long-term goals by investing, and so I was able to convince myself to relinquish some of that control and take on some risk."

"It's like your value around financial security is at war with itself."

"What do you mean?"

"Well, you crave stability."

"Understatement of the century," she joked.

I laughed with her and continued, "And up until now, you've given yourself that security by having total control and 100% predictable outcomes with your money. Paying down debt, predictable. Saving money in cash accounts, predictable. All of which made sense for that time in your life. Paying down debt is like paying back the past. Saving up for emergencies is like saving for the present. But, now, we are done planning the short run. This $10,000 is earmarked for your long-term retirement. Over the long run, 100% predictable outcomes, like a 1% savings account, don't usually exist. There has to be some element of risk or else there's no opportunity for growth."

"Exactly. I'm trying to future-proof myself, and it's anxiety-inducing either way. I feel like I either have to sell everything and get it back to cash so I get that control and guaranteed predictability. Or I can do nothing, have anxiety over the complete lack of predictability while it drops daily, and have absolutely no control over my future. Both options feel so extreme."

I typed the following on a Word document on our shared screen. I read them out loud as I typed.

**Option 1:** Do nothing. Keep the money fully invested and carry on investing the $250 a month.

**Option 2:** Sell everything. Go to cash and move all future money to cash.

"I want you to assign short-term predictability and long-term predictability to each option on a scale of 0 to 5, with 0 being no predictability and 5 being guaranteed predictability."

"Okay," she agreed.

"Let's start with Option 2. If you sell all your investments and move them to cash, plus you move the $250 a month of future savings to cash, how much predictability do you have in the short term?"

"How long is the short term?"

"The next 2 to 3 years."

"A five?" She was asking.

"How so?"

"Well, it's in cash so it's guaranteed. There's total predictability. No risk."

Beside Option 2 I typed a 5/5 for short-term predictability.

"What about Option 1: Do nothing?"

"Uh," she paused. "Maybe a 1."

"Why?"

"Because it's all invested and I can't control stock market risk. It could go up tomorrow or down."

"Then why don't you give it a zero?"

"*Hmmmm.* I think because maybe . . ." She shrugged her shoulders. "Maybe I hope there's a degree of predictability? Like, there's some sort of method to the madness of capitalism? A sort of, what came before will happen again? And that this type of volatility is normal."

"What about long-term predictability?" I asked. "Anything about the long run that feels within your control or predictable for Option 2?"

"For Option 2, it feels really predictable still. Like a 5/5 because it's in cash. There's still no risk," she cut herself off. "Okay, there's risk, but it's predictable."

"What risk?" I asked, knowingly.

She smiled. "Sitting in cash, earning interest below the rate of inflation, is a risk over the long run. So it's predictable, because the outcome is guaranteed, but it totally stands in the way of any chance at long-term growth for retirement."

"So in the long run, Option 2 has 5/5 short and long-term predictability, but over the long term, it violates your deciding value of financial security."

"Exactly. It feels safe but not smart."

"What about Option 1? What predictability do you have over the long run?"

She scrunched her face. "Well, in February I accepted the idea that there was risk or unpredictable volatility in exchange for long-term growth. I felt very confident in it because of the fact that, for better or worse, stock markets have overall gone up over time and corrections and booms and busts are normal. So, to me, in a strange way, the long run of investing seems more predictable. Like a 3/5. I know I don't have control over it, but I'm less scared of it. It's like I believe that the long run it will be okay, but the short-term volatility scares me."

"Investing can feel really scary at times."

"I just hate the short-term lack of control. It makes me feel like the long run is at risk because I can't control my way out of it. I just have to surrender to it and that's why I can't sleep. The short-term volatility makes me feel like I'm being stupid with my money because I can't control any of it."

"To summarize, Option 2 is entirely predictable, but not really an option because the long term violates your deciding values. Option 1, the long term feels okay, but the short term is clashing with your need to feel in control, or your deciding value of financial security in the short run.

"Yes." She nodded. "I feel trapped. Like I'm screwed either way. I have no good option."

"Well, that's not entirely true," I said.

"What do you mean?"

"You came in with these two extreme options. Sell everything and have anxiety. Or do nothing and have anxiety. But I think there are more."

"I'm intrigued at the prospect of a third option," she said.

"Good." I grinned. "Option 3 is keep the $10,000, now $7,800, and the $250 a month of new savings, but each month reassess your risk tolerance. If you feel nervous, you can move the $250 a month to cash."

She waited a moment before she spoke, as if she was fully calculating all the ways this option could fail. "*Hmmm,* that's interesting," she said.

"Isn't it?" I raised an eyebrow.

"Let me get this straight. I keep the original $10,000 fully invested."

"Yes."

"But each month I can choose to invest the new $250 or put the $250 to cash with no risk."

"Yes."

"So I still get to save money each month, but the decision to invest or not feels smaller."

"How do you mean?"

"Well, making a decision based on $250 feels like lower stakes than the decision to invest my life savings. I know it's the same decision, but framing it this way, each month, feels less intimidating."

"Why do you think that is?"

"Well, I get to control where that $250 goes. If I feel scared, I can save it to cash. If I don't, I can move it to investments. But, either way, I can change my mind the next month. It's not all or nothing."

"Can you rate Option 3 for both short- and long-term predictability?"

"In the short run, it feels 5/5 control because even if it's invested, I get to choose that. That's within my control. The stock market isn't, but the decision to invest is. And if I choose to invest it, then I'm accepting the short-term volatility. It's on my terms, and it's not forever. I'm not deciding to never invest or to only invest."

"What about the long-term predictability?"

"Same as Option 1. A 3/5. I mean, I know that the stock market is totally out of my control, but hopefully there's some long-term growth that doesn't feel out of the realm of normal."

"Does this option violate your deciding value of financial security?"

"Not at all. In the short run, I feel like it gives me financial security because I can move the new monthly contributions to cash without guilt. But I don't jeopardize my chance at long-term growth and feel stupid for cashing out at the potential bottom by selling the initial investment." She laughed. "It's upholding my need for long-term growth while giving me some short-term control."

"It's the illusion of short-term control," I offered.

"I love it. Like a control placebo. It's a slow acclimatization of risk that feels like I'm doing it on my terms and doesn't make me feel reckless for panic-selling."

"Exactly." I smiled. "And stop checking your account every day."

She laughed. "Why?"

"Since you don't plan on cashing out the initial investment, checking the value every day is only going to freak you out. There's no helpful decision-making information there for you. All it's going to do is mire you in panic mode all over again. Do yourself a favour. Take the app off your phone."

She laughed. "That will be hard."

"Yes, but if you truly want to harness this positive outlook, don't look at it."

"I get it. I'm deleting the app now," she said, looking down at her phone.

"So how do you feel about everything?"

She took a big breath and closed her eyes. "Calmer," she said. "It feels good to have a plan and to know that I can pull the trigger on the new savings when I need to."

"If the whole initial $10,000 goes to zero in the next month, would you look back at this moment and say, *I made the best decision I could on that day given the facts I had?*"

She thought about that. "I would," she said confidently. "I actually think I'd regret that less than if I cashed it out and things went up again."

"Beautiful. That's where you need to be. The long run is so unpredictable that all we really have is a measure of control over the short run. Making decisions based on your deciding values for the short-term predictability is about as good as it gets. It gives you confidence in your choices and allows you to sleep at night, knowing that you made the best decision you could at the time and for all the right reasons."

For the record, as I write this, her investments have fully recovered and are worth over $10,250. She is very glad she didn't cash out when her stocks were low. She also knows that it's possible that she will have downturns again in the future, but now she knows how to make no-regret decisions when that happens.

Trying to control what life will look like 10 years from now is a fool's errand. All you can do in the short run is keep putting one predictable foot in front of the other and ensuring that your values are upheld. That way, you'll know that you're always choosing a life that makes you happy.

## HOMEWORK: ASSIGN SHORT-TERM PREDICTABILITY AND LONG-TERM PREDICTABILITY

**Step 1:** Outline all your options.

**Step 2:** Assign short-term predictability on a scale of 0 to 5, with 0 being no predictability and 5 being guaranteed predictability. How likely is it that you can control the outcome over the next 1 to 2 years?

**Step 3:** Assign long-term predictability on a scale of 0 to 5, with 0 being no predictability and 5 being guaranteed predictability. How likely is it that you can control the outcome of your decision after 2 years? This number is usually low since life is random and so much is out of our control.

**Step 4:** Choose your best option. If the option you choose has zero predictability in the short term or the long term, that's okay. It just means you're taking a flyer. Make that decision with your eyes open. If you chose an option with some degree of short-term predictability, this gives you some short-term control, which can help you when you look back, even if the situation doesn't work out.

# CHAPTER 8:

## Determining How and When to Pivot Your Plans

So now that you've discovered your core and deciding values, you understand why the best way to make no-regret decisions is to ensure that every choice you make while in a decision crisis honours those deciding values and offers even a small amount of control or predictability in the short term with decision predictability. This is how you know you've made the best decisions possible at the time, given the information and constraints you're facing. You want to be able to look back and say, *I wouldn't change a thing, even if the outcome isn't ideal.*

But what happens when there are simply no guarantees? When there isn't even an ounce of short-term, let alone long-term, predictability? What happens when you are dealing with extreme uncertainty and very high stakes? Unimaginably high. Like, life-and-death high.

What happens to the Decision Crisis Playbook then?

The answer is simple: The Decision Crisis Playbook gets thrown out the window.

Extreme stakes combined with zero predictability means the Decision Crisis Playbook can't work. The only way to make no-regret decisions when you're in this kind of intense situation is to know when you'll need to pivot your plans to buy yourself more time and figure out when you need to throw in the towel altogether.

Most of the decision crises that I come across in my day-to-day work have high stakes. We've already talked about many of them: divorce, job loss, a global pandemic, and even the death of a loved one.

While I'm not a grief counsellor or a mental health worker, when people come to me after a major life-changing event or when they're in a period of transition, it's because they need to make decisions. Big and complex decisions. My job is to help people move through the decision-making process. When you're in a decision crisis, regardless of how difficult the situation is, you have no other choice but to keep making choices.

The same holds true when the stakes are literally life and death and there is zero predictability in the outcome. A terminal illness diagnosis for yourself or a loved one leaves you reeling with no guarantees, no predictability, nothing solid to hold on to at all, yet financial decisions have to be made.

Riding the IVF rollercoaster has similar stakes as well, with a complete lack of predictability and no guarantees. Emotions are running high, everything is unknown, yet you need to make major financial decisions.

In both instances, people are living in a world that is 50% magic and 50% science. And no doctor can give predictions because every medical journey is completely personal.

Given the lack of predictability in such situations, it's not surprising that I often hear the same things from clients who are on these very different journeys.

"We are going to keep trying until we can't anymore," they'll say.

*Until we can't anymore.* But when will that be?

That's the question they want me to answer.

When people say this to me they are looking for a boundary. The "I Can't Anymore" boundary.

But the truth is, I can't give them the answer. Only *they* know where that line is. All I can do is support their decision and help outline where other life plans may need to pivot to make room or to buy more time for their journey to run its course. That's it.

When it comes to decision-making, constraints exist whether we want to acknowledge them or not. It's naïve to think you can make good, values-based decisions without recognizing the constraints that go with them. These constraints are *time* and *money*. Money is the reason I have client meetings with people in a decision crisis on a weekly basis.

I believe we shouldn't resent constraints—they can be very useful when dealing with uncertainty. They can provide a road map where there isn't one. Bring things sharply into focus. In the Decision Crisis Playbook, you can use constraints to ensure that you don't have regrets when you're on the other side of your decision crisis.

Time and money constraints help map your decision-making in two ways: First, they provide *pivot points*. Pivot points are when your best-case scenario didn't play out and you have to change other life plans in order to buy time or put more money toward whatever goal you are chasing. For example, imagine that you inherited $100,000. Your best-case scenario was to do a major renovation in your home, which was quoted at $60,000; purchase a new car for $30,000; and save $10,000 to take your family on a very special trip, a trip that really means something to you. That's the ideal case.

But what if the quotes for the renovation all come out around $75,000 to $80,000 for the work you want to get done? Then you need to make decisions about how to reduce the scope of the renovation to keep it under $60,000 or keep going with the original renovation plan and either give up your special trip, buy a cheaper car, or don't buy a car at all. The point is, you have options, even if the best-case scenario didn't work out. Financial constraints are forcing you to pivot your plan somewhere. If your deciding value is around family time and the trip really is special to you, then maybe you keep the renovation plans as they are, and keep the vacation, and pivot your plans away from the car. Maybe you don't need a new car for another 3 to 5 years, and you can wait. This is how constraints work to create pivot points. You pivot your plans, you keep going forward with the plan that honours your deciding values, and you give up something less important to you. The classic "something's gotta give."

Time and money constraints also create time and money guardrails. Guardrails are different than pivot points. Guardrails mean there are no more options. You're out of time or you're out of money. Guardrails suck sometimes.

In our renovation example, imagine that you've already pivoted away from the car. You're mid-renovation and the cost of the renovation is skyrocketing. The renovation will likely end up costing $100,000, and you have already torn up the floors so you have to keep going. You're stuck. You have to allocate all of the money to the renovation. One of your money guardrails was that you promised yourself that you'd never go into debt again after digging yourself out of debt only a few years ago. That means you're out of money. You have to put it toward the renovation and, therefore, you're forced to give up the really special family trip. There's no other choice. That's a guardrail. When you've pivoted as much as you can, it's time to make the hardest decision.

I'm going to tell you a story about my client Sarah. Sarah is married to Nicole. They knew they wanted to have children from the first date. They knew that Sarah was going to carry the baby. They knew that science was already going to be involved in their fertility journey. They expected that. What they didn't expect was a heart-wrenching 4-year fertility journey, 6 failed rounds of IVF, the hidden price tag of IVF, and the way their other life goals and plans would have to pivot several times over the course of their journey. (I just

159

want to take a moment to let you know that this story has a happy ending. You can exhale now.)

## MEET SARAH AND NICOLE
RELATIONSHIP STATUS: Married
AGES: 37 and 39
CHILDREN: Two fertilized eggs in storage

Sarah and Nicole had scheduled a planning meeting with me but called me beforehand. On this call, they told me they had just found out that the third round of IVF treatments they had tried had failed.

"I can't even imagine," I offered solemnly. "I'm so sorry for your loss."

We had booked their planning meeting months earlier when they first started IVF. This meeting was supposed to be for babyproofing their finances and plotting out Sarah's parental leave. When they told me the news about their third failed round, I asked if they wanted to cancel that upcoming meeting, but they said no.

"Okay," I said, "but I need to give you a heads up about something before you come in."

"Let me guess," Sarah said flatly. "You're pregnant."

"I am," I said softly.

Silence.

"Hello?" I said into the phone after an awkward length of time had passed.

"We're here," Nicole said.

"I didn't want it to be a surprise when you saw me," I said. Then added, "It's okay if you want to punch me in the face."

I was, obviously, being beyond sarcastic, but I was looking for a shocking way to let Sarah know that I anticipated she might have a strong and negative reaction to my news. I heard her giggle slightly on the other end of the receiver.

"Thank you for the offer," she said. "It's fine. People get pregnant. Just not me, apparently."

I didn't say anything.

"I guess you're *allowed* to be happy," she said with mock authority, and I knew we were going to be fine. "I'm probably going to mute you on social media while you're knocked up."

"I totally get it," I said seriously.

"Thank you for the heads up, though."

They had been my clients for almost a decade. We bordered on good pals by this point. When they came in for their planning meeting, we hugged.

"What do you want to get out of this meeting today so that when you leave, you're able to say, *Yep, that's exactly what we needed.*"

Neither of them said anything.

"Sarah, why did you want to keep this appointment?" I asked.

"I don't even know how to make decisions anymore. I feel like we make life-altering decisions every f*cking day. I'm so exhausted." She slouched in her chair. "And hormonal."

I nodded.

"Nicole?"

"The same," she said, and I noticed that her hand hadn't left Sarah's since they got there.

"Okay," I said. "I'd like permission to ask some tough questions."

They both smiled.

"Our whole life is a tough question," Sarah replied.

I smiled. "What's your worst-case scenario here?"

Nicole didn't say a word. She just squeezed Sarah's hand.

Sarah inhaled sharply, then let out a long breath. "That all of this is for nothing. That we've wasted years of our lives in this hormone-hell where I literally cry over spilled milk. I worry that our finances can't recover from this and it never even works. It's all I think about."

I nodded.

"Nicole?"

She thought for a moment, then cleared her throat. "That Sarah has regrets."

Sarah looked at Nicole. "That's so cute, boo," she said and gave a playful pout.

"It's true," Nicole said seriously, not allowing Sarah to brush it off with humour. "You've been such a trooper through all of this. No matter how this plays out, I don't want you to have regret." They hugged. This kind of love was straight out of a movie. I will never forget that moment.

"Can I ask a potentially silly question?" I asked.

"Sure," Sarah replied.

"What's your best-case scenario?"

They both laughed, almost nervously.

"*Um,* a baby? Like tomorrow. No more IVF rounds. No more acupuncture, no more time off work, no more meditation." Sarah shook her head. "I want off the ride but not without the baby part."

Nicole agreed.

I smiled. "The baby part."

"Yep," Sarah said.

"I think it's interesting that the financial security piece only shows up in your worst-case scenario. Not the best *and* the worst."

"What do you mean?" Nicole asked.

"Usually I see deciding values mirrored in both. Best-case scenario is your ideal core values being honoured. In your worst-case scenario, the same core values are being violated. For you, the value of having a family is in both. But financial security only shows up in your worst case. So maybe it's not a deciding value but rather a financial constraint that we have to deal with."

They thought about that for a moment before Sarah spoke.

"I think it's important to say that yes, having a baby is our number-one goal, but it can't be the only deciding value because what if it doesn't work out?"

I didn't say anything.

"What do you mean?" Nicole asked.

"Well, if we can't get pregnant, I don't want our whole life to feel like second prize forever. Like we are settling, as if having a baby is the only way to live our values."

Nicole bit her lower lip but nodded.

Sarah looked at me. "Sorry, IVF has made us very super-stitious. It's like even talking about it now feels like somehow we are jinxing the process."

"Don't apologize," I said.

"So if having the baby isn't our number-one value, what is?" Nicole asked.

"I think it's our number-one *goal*," Sarah said.

Nicole nodded. "Okay, that makes sense."

"Sarah?" I asked gently. "What needs to happen so that you don't regret anything even if you don't reach that number-one goal?"

She put her head back and looked at the ceiling. "I don't even know." Then she faced Nicole. "I think that we tried everything we possibly could. No stone unturned."

"No clinic untried," Nicole added with a smile.

"Hope," I offered.

They nodded in unison without saying anything.

"I think hope is a core value," I said.

Sarah spoke first. "Yes. For me, I think I want to, no, I *need* to maintain optimism. To keep going through this. To believe that life can be good no matter what happens and to give me the strength to keep making these insane choices every month. It's terrifying."

"Me too," Nicole said.

"What, specifically, is terrifying?"

"The anxiety that all this emotional trauma and money are spent for no reason," Sarah said. "Also, our relationship. I don't want to jeopardize that."

They both nodded.

I picked up my marker and started to write. "Okay. I hear two values here and one constraint so far."

| CORE VALUES | CONSTRAINTS |
| --- | --- |
| • Hope for their future together (with or without baby)<br>• Love relationship | • Money |

I showed them. "Do these feel like mutually shared values?" They read them over and nodded.

"In that order?" I asked. "With *Hope for your future together* trumping all others to some degree?"

"Yes," Sarah said.

"Same," Nicole agreed.

"This is important to know."

"Why?" Sarah asked.

"These are your deciding values," I said. "*Hope* and *love*. And we know that money isn't a value, only a constraint. So yes, we have to take it into account when making decisions, but we aren't going to make choices to honour it, merely work around or with it.

What is the next big choice you have to make?" I asked.

"It's monthly," Sarah said. "Every time I get my period we have to decide if we want to go through IVF again, or do we want to wait and recover from our grief? Do I want to start injecting myself with expensive drugs that make me feel crazy and cost a fortune? How much more *effing* pineapple can I eat?" She and Nicole laughed.

"Okay, so when you're trying to make decisions with no predictability, no guarantees, and extreme stakes, you need to make your choices purely on what honours your deciding values until you either have to change plans or change course."

Five years before, long before their fertility journey began, Sarah and Nicole came in to see me to make some life plans. Together, we mapped out a 5-year plan for Nicole to go back to school and get her master's degree while they saved up to buy a house. They also wanted to start trying for a baby. Because Sarah made the larger income, they also planned to save enough to allow her to take an entire year off for parental leave. We called their joint savings their "baby savings account." On paper, they were set. They had all the pieces in place.

Three years into that plan, after five rounds of IVF, their baby savings account was empty.

"No one talks about all the extra costs of IVF," Sarah said. "It's like our budget is a constantly moving target."

I nodded.

"The procedure is covered by health care, but none of the extra costs are covered. Acupuncture, drugs, therapy, supplements, extra testing, storage of eggs. It goes on and on. We tallied it up. Over the last 3 years, we've spent $25,000." She was slouched in her chair, hands in the pocket of her hoodie.

"We need to know if we can keep going or not," Sarah said flatly. "We are out of money in the baby savings account."

I shifted in my chair. "It's not up to me to decide if you should keep going."

"I know that," she said, sharply. "But if we are going to keep going, I need to know how we do it because we are out of the money that was allocated for this."

"Not really," I said. "You still both have your jobs, and you have savings in other accounts."

Sarah was shaking her head no. "Those are for Nicole's tuition and our down payment fund."

I nodded and took a big breath. "So you've reached a pivot point."

"What's that?" Nicole asked.

"In a nutshell, a pivot point is when your best-case scenario didn't work out, but you still have choices. It doesn't mean you have to throw in the towel altogether, but something else in your life has to change in order to keep going."

They didn't say anything.

"Let me ask you something," I continued. "Would you go bankrupt in order to buy yourself more time?"

Sarah let out a laugh. "We probably *will* go bankrupt at this rate."

"That's not even remotely true right now," I corrected. "There are still a lot of options. But in all seriousness, if you blew through every dollar to your names, took on debt, and had to file for bankruptcy, would you do it?"

"No. For sure not," Sarah said.

"Nicole?"

"Me neither. I don't want us to be destitute," she replied.

"So baby at *almost* all costs," Sarah said and smiled.

"Exactly. Let's work backward from there."

I opened their file.

"Here are some of the life plans from your best-case scenario that you have been working toward from our meeting 5 years ago."

1.  Have a baby
2.  Nicole finishes her master's
3.  Sarah takes a full year off for parental leave
4.  Buy a home

"The option to keep trying for baby isn't gone, but you're at a pivot point where the financial constraints are forcing you to pivot your plans."

Nicole nodded. "The point when something's gotta give."

Sarah's eyes teared up. "I hate that something has to give!"

"What do you hate about the idea of pivoting?" I asked gently.

Tears fell in earnest now. "It's the not knowing. All this sacrificing of our plans on the chance that magic and science will do its thing." She looked at Nicole. "How far do we go?"

She wiped her eyes with the back of her sweater.

"We go until we can't," Nicole said quietly.

"When's that?" Sarah asked. "Where's *can't*?"

They both looked at me. It was such an intense moment.

"That's not up to me," I said. "I wish I could."

"I know," Sarah said, wiping her eyes.

"I can help plot out some red flags, your pivot points, along the way so you know when you do have to change plans."

"On the way to *can't*," Sarah said.

"In a way, yes," I said. "Pivot points are times when you have to change your ideal life plans because time or money constraints exist. Pivot points means that there are still options. You're not at *can't* yet."

"Where's *can't*?" Nicole asked quietly.

"It's when you reach the point where there are no more options. There's no more time and no more money that you can put toward your goals. I call those lines in the sand time and money guardrails."

"We can't keep going forever," Sarah said.

"I know," Nicole replied.

"I don't want us to be destitute," Sarah said.

"What does that mean for you?" I asked.

She shrugged. "I think it means Nicole wouldn't go to school, we'd never own a house, and we'd have so much debt that we'd never save a cent."

Nicole nodded.

"What if you won the lottery tomorrow and money wasn't a constraint? How long do you think you'd go for? Forever?"

They looked at each other and laughed awkwardly.

"I hope not," Sarah said with a smile that broke the tension.

"Your body, your call," Nicole said.

Sarah took a deep breath in and let it out slowly. "Realistically, I wouldn't want to be giving birth after 45. It's not 45 as an age, lots of women have kids after 45, but for me, it will have been over a decade of trying at that point. It would just be too many years for me. So much of my life spent obsessed with the lining of my uterus. I don't want that to go on for more than a decade, even if that means no baby."

"So 8 more years. If money was no object."

They agreed.

"So now we have one time guardrail," I said, writing *After a decade* on the page before turning back to them. "You told me once that IVF costs you about $10,000 a year."

They nodded.

"So $80,000 ($10,000 x 8 years) is what's at stake here financially."

"That's terrifying," Sarah said.

"Let's math it out," I said. "In order to keep trying for the next 8 years, the entire $60,000 in your down payment fund would go toward fertility as well as the money earmarked for Nicole's schooling ($20,000). Those are your two additional pivot points, since you've already pivoted once."

"How so?" Nicole asked.

"We've already depleted the parental leave fund, in the baby savings account," Sarah said. "We've already changed our ideal plans."

Nicole nodded. "Right."

"But," I said, "did you do it without regrets? It sounds like it wasn't even a question. Trying IVF and honouring your deciding values were much higher on your list of priorities than having a fully funded parental leave."

Sarah shook her head. "The whole idea of a fully funded parental leave seems so unbelievably unimportant and privileged at this point."

"Spending the money in the baby savings account *was* a pivot point," I explained. "When you reached it, you still had options, and you pivoted away from your ideal plan to make room for your IVF journey to continue. So now, we just have to figure out how to keep doing that until you reach a money guardrail." I picked up the marker again. "So at this point, which would you prioritize more over the next 8 years: home ownership or Nicole's school?"

"School. Hands down," Sarah piped up. She looked right at Nicole. "That's happening no matter what."

"Nicole, do you agree?" She nodded, and I continued. "Then you've decided together that you are you willing to spend $10,000 of the down payment fund to keep Nicole in school and keep trying for baby."

"Yes," they both said at the same time.

"That felt like a no-brainer," Nicole said with a smile.

"What about spending the entire $60,000 on IVF?" I asked gently.

Sarah cringed. "I don't want to make this choice yet."

"Tell me about that."

"Agreeing to spend the *whole* amount right now feels like we are saying no to our dream of home ownership."

"That's why it's called a pivot point," I said. "It's where the ideal life plans have to change because constraints exist."

"I don't know if I'm comfortable with that," Sarah said to Nicole.

Nicole shrugged. "It doesn't mean we can't ever buy a house. It means we wouldn't buy one in the next 8 years."

"Right," Sarah said nodding. "But I feel like even if that

account went down to $30,000, we'd have to rethink our home ownership plan anyways because we'd spent so much of it already."

"That's true," Nicole agreed.

"And if you did pivot to renting and spent the whole amount," I said, "that would only get you to 5 more years. At that point, you'd need to go into debt."

"I guess you're going to ask, how much debt?" Nicole said.

I nodded. "You said earlier, you don't want to be destitute or unable to save. You can still save over the next few years so it may never come to this, but is there an amount of debt that you'd feel comfortable with taking on in order to make room for your IVF journey to keep going?"

"I think one extra year. The $10,000 fully paid for with debt, would be fine," Sarah said. She looked at Nicole. "I wouldn't care because we could pay that $10,000 off over a couple of years."

Nicole agreed.

"And if it grew to more than that?" I asked, carefully.

"No," Sarah said. "Hard no."

"I agree," Nicole added.

"So that feels like you've reached a money guardrail. A *can't anymore* place," I said.

"I think so," Sarah said. "If we've given up our entire $60,000 down payment fund and taken on $10,000 in debt, and there's still no baby, I'd say I'm done. I'd regret taking on more debt than that."

I presented their pivot points:

1. When baby savings account is $0, must decide whether to pivot to Sarah not taking full year off work. (Already done!)
2. When the down payment fund is at $30,000, must decide whether to pivot to renting instead of owning for longer.
3. When all savings are gone, must pivot to taking on debt.

Next, I showed them their time and money guardrails:

**Time guardrail:** After a decade of trying
**Money guardrail:** When $10,000 in debt

We all looked at the list solemnly.

"That's a big list," I said.

"Yes," they both agreed.

"Do you think you'd have any regrets if you reached either of your guardrails?"

They looked at each other.

"No," Nicole said. "These really do feel like guardrails so we don't go off the end of a cliff. In a way, it makes me feel safe. Like we aren't out there without a plan."

"If 8 years from now we had no savings," Sarah said, "and we were $10,000 in the hole and still renting, I'd be sad but, no, I don't think I'd have regret." She turned to Nicole. "Wow, babe, we *really* want a baby."

We all burst out laughing. It felt good to laugh after such an intense meeting.

I am happy to report that Sarah and Nicole had a baby girl (Darcy) and are grateful for sleepless nights and baby vomit. Nicole has completed her master's degree as well, and they managed to accomplish all that without going into debt. But they did have to make some pivot decisions.

They dipped into their down payment fund until it was down to $10,000 (original plan was to go no lower than $30,000). After using $20,000 on IVF, they decided that it would be better for Sarah to take the full year of parental leave because Nicole is still new at her job. So they decided to use the last $10,000 of the down payment fund to pay for the difference in income while Sarah was off work. Essentially, they pivoted away from their home ownership plans for now. But they didn't have to go into debt and they didn't hit a time or money guardrail. That was something to celebrate.

We had a quick phone check-in after Darcy was born. I asked how they felt about their decision to keep renting without knowing when home ownership would be back on the table.

"We don't care," Sarah said almost blissfully. "Darcy is here. Nothing else matters."

"It's also not off the table forever," Nicole added. "Just for now. And if there's anything we've learned through this entire process, it's that we are stubborn as hell when we want to achieve something."

I was so happy for them.

• , •

When you are making decisions about goals with extremely high emotional and financial stakes combined with extreme uncertainty, even the smallest decision will seem fraught. By using your time and money constraints to create pivot points, you can help navigate the uncertainty and give yourself the freedom not to agonize over every decision you'll need to make along the road.

## HOMEWORK: CREATE PIVOT POINTS

**Step 1:** Make a list of your life goals that you worry are (potentially) at stake of not happening or that might change if your ideal scenario doesn't play out. This can be anything from giving up travel plans, to applying for other jobs, to starting a new career, retiring, buying a home, having a baby, etc.

**Step 2:** Identify your pivot points. At what point do each of the plans/goals in Step 1 become threatened? These are your pivot points. This could be an amount of time that has passed or an amount of money that is reached. The pivot point is the stage at which your other life plans must shift to either make way for something new or to continue seeking your ideal outcome.

# CHAPTER 9:

## Creating Time and
## Money Guardrails

Even after you've established your deciding values, created micro goals and timelines, and established pivot points when you're in a decision crisis, you may be wondering how long you can wait or how much you can spend trying to get your best-case scenario.

How do you decide when you need to leave your partner? Quit your job? Start a new business? Sign the divorce papers? Buy a house? Sell a house? Have kids? Don't have kids? Start dating? Never date again? Retire? Not retire?

We know that pivot points are places where you need to alter your life plans because you need more time or things cost more money than originally planned in your best-case scenario. But hitting a pivot point means you still have options. There's still time and there's still money. You just have to alter some other plans.

Reaching a time or money guardrail is different, though. It's the end of the road. There are no more options. You are out of time or you are out of money. You have to make a hard choice.

This is how your time and money guardrails help you make no-regret decisions. They light a fire under you and give you a safe and worry-free chance to go after your best-case scenario and to continue pivoting your plans until you have to make a hard decision to stop.

An even simpler way of looking at it is to think of your money guardrail as the amount of money that represents the line between *spend without regret* and *stop*.

Similarly, your time guardrail represents a deadline. It's the difference between *keep going* and *stop*. Sometimes, a time guardrail is decided for you. For instance, if you get a letter from the government demanding a response within 30 days, well, your time guardrail is 30 days. You don't have a choice. You can push it off until the very last day, but ultimately, you still have to decide within 30 days what you're going to do and come up with a plan of action.

Sometimes money guardrails are decided for you as well. A great example would be purchasing a home. Let's say you have $100,000 for a down payment and have been approved for a $500,000 mortgage. You can afford to buy a house for $600,000. Not $601,000. Even if you wanted to, you can't. Your money guardrail is set by what the bank will lend you. The boundary has been set for you.

If there isn't a hard deadline or set financial boundary, you need to create them yourself.

To figure out your time guardrail, ask yourself, *If money weren't a constraint (you win the lottery), would you keep going forever?* If yes, you don't have a time guardrail. If no, when would you stop? That's your time guardrail. When you run out of time. Sometimes this is put on you by someone else or a hard deadline. Other times, you have to make one yourself. At what point would you feel regret? How long would it take until you resented how much time it took?

It's the same with your money guardrail. How much money would you spend until you regretted it? Usually, you can start by asking yourself how you'd feel if you went bankrupt.

Figuring out how much money and time you can afford to spend without regret is an integral part of your decision-making process because your guardrails are the last line of defence. They force you to make a hard decision when you must consider throwing in the towel.

The good news is that until you reach your time or money guardrail, you can keep spending time and money in pursuit of your best-case scenario without guilt or anxiety. You're safe to chase down your best-case scenario. You may hit some pivot points along the way, but that's not the same as stopping. You still have options and you're still pursuing your major goal. It's not until you hit one of your guardrails that the game is over and the goal you've been pursuing is officially at an end.

Trying to make decisions without guardrails makes the whole Decision Crisis Playbook feel like it's fraught with danger. If you're not sure you can afford something, no matter what you do, you'll feel like you're lighting yourself on fire financially. And if you don't have a firm deadline, every day that you put off making a decision will be riddled with guilt for procrastinating.

With guardrails, however, you can relax. Carry on in pursuit of your goals and, if you hit your guardrail, you'll know it's time to change course completely. When you hit a guardrail, it means things didn't work out. It's a hard, hard decision to change course. But you won't regret changing course because you'll know you've tried your best to get what you want, but now you've hit the limit where it's no longer safe to proceed.

Even if your worst-case scenario plays out, you should be able to look back and say, *I wouldn't change a thing. I gave it all I could and called it when I needed to.*

Hitting one of your guardrails sucks. It means your best-case scenario didn't play out. It means that your values are at war with each other and you now have to make decisions—hard decisions that you don't want to make but you can't put off any longer.

This is story about dreams and time and money.

## MEET ANNE AND JOHN
AGES: 55 and 58
RELATIONSHIP STATUS: Married
CHILDREN: 2 (ages 25 and 26)

Anne and John have been married for 30 years and have owned a business together—a high-end men's clothing store

specializing in imported goods from England and Europe—
for 25 years. John started the store decades ago after immi-
grating to Canada from England. He told me he opened the
shop because he still wanted to feel like an Englishman. Just
after they were married, Anne left her career as a nurse to
join forces with John, to save on employee costs.

The store has been an icon since the 90s. John is well
known in the community, and they've gotten a lot of media
coverage over the years. But here's the big secret: For all
the headlines, press, and history, the store has been failing
financially for the last 5 years. With drastic increases in
commercial rent over the last 10 years and the rise of online
shopping, they just can't keep up.

Anne and John first came to see me 2 years ago. When
they arrived, it was immediately obvious that John didn't
want to be there. He was cold, aloof, and sat far back from the
table with his arms crossed. The only thing he asked about
in the first 10 minutes of the meeting was my qualifications.
I knew I had my work cut out for me.

I was, however, prepared for this. You see, the information they had given me before their session was very telling.

When asked about their goals, here's what they said:

**Anne:** We need to retire. It's possible with the money
we have saved, plus we could rent out our basement
apartment. The business is losing so much money.
We only have $60,000 left on our business line of
credit. We've worked too hard to lose everything
now. I don't want any more sleepless nights.

**John:** I'd like to invest some money into the shop so I can have more time to work *on* the business rather than *in* the business. I think we need about $40,000 to update our online retail store and hire a digital marketing consultant. I have applied for a business loan to help with this. I would also like to hire a manager so I can work in a more strategic way.

This couple was clearly not aligned. They had very different emotional and perceived financial stakes. Anne was afraid that their personal financial safety would be at risk if they kept the business going. John was afraid they would be selling themselves short of potential income by shutting the store down.

I grew up in a family business, and I know that when the owners are not aligned on future goals things can be tense. Even more so when the owners are family. You don't leave the tension at the office. It bleeds into breakfast, lunch, and dinner. These two needed to find some common ground— and compromises.

After introductions and small talk, I waded into the important issues, delicately.

"This is a really complex situation. I'd love for each of you to tell me what you want to get out of our session today."

Anne went first. "For starters, we need to run some scenarios to see what our life looks like if we close the business. I think we are in okay shape financially on the personal front, but we are not breaking even at the store. We haven't been for years. We keep going further and further into corporate debt. I'm worried that we will have to start putting personal money into the business just to pay rent and payroll. We've had a good run, but I think it's time to—"

John cut her off. "You make it sound like we have borrowed hundreds of thousands and that I'm just gambling our money away." He looked at me for the first time. "We've used $75,000 of our business line of credit over the last 5 years. We have been running a $15,000 annual operating loss, and she's acting like the last 30 years have been an economic wasteland."

"I didn't say that," she said.

"You may as well have," he shot back.

"No," she said in an overly controlled way. "I'm saying that we had a good run. A great run, but it's time to look at the signs. The writing is on the wall, but you're so far out on a limb you can't even see it. I'm angry that all our hard work now feels like it is dribbling away."

"No," he said. "You're angry because you hate doing the bookkeeping and the operations. Admit it."

"I do hate it."

"Then quit!" he replied, angrily.

"We can't afford for me to quit!" she yelled.

He looked at me again, leaning forward. "Listen, if you want to run numbers about retirement that's fine. But I'll tell you this now: There's more money on the table here, but she's too tired and has no risk tolerance whatsoever. We don't need to close; we need to grow. I'm the one seeing clearly."

He pointed at her with his thumb, without looking at her. "*She's* the one out on a limb."

"Okay, everyone!" I put my hands up in the air. "That's enough."

It's rare for full-blown fights to break out in my office, but I felt like this one needed to happen. Plus it gave me a clear picture of what was happening between them and a sense of the emotional stakes.

Anne and John took a couple of deep settling breaths and sat back in their chairs, muttering apologies.

"It's no problem," I said. "You're both scared."

"I'm not–" John began.

"Let her speak," Anne said, irritated.

"To me, it sounds like you're both scared," I continued. "But of very different things. It sounds like Anne is afraid that keeping the business open will start impacting your personal finances and put your retirement in jeopardy." I looked at Anne. "That sound right?"

She nodded.

I turned to John. "I know you're not worried about your retirement. To me, it sounds like you're afraid of missing out on future opportunities within the business that will give you more money than you have now and allow you to retire even more comfortably."

"Something like that," he said.

This guy was tricky.

"What I see is that you both have different stakes around the same decision."

"Which decision?" Anne asked. "It feels like there are so many."

"After listening to you both, I'd say the main decision is whether you close the business or keep it open."

"There are so many more decisions than that," John said.

"Not really," I said bluntly. "Ultimately, all the other decisions." I listed them off on my fingers. "Hire someone, have Anne quit, invest in digital marketing, start an online store, etc., are all decisions that come *after* you've both decided to keep the business open. If you both decide to close, those decisions don't need to be made."

John started to speak then closed his mouth. I could tell he was pondering. Looking for a hole in my logic.

"Yes, but aren't those factors all part of the decision to stay open?" Anne asked.

"We don't know yet," I said.

They looked at each other skeptically. It was the first bit of camaraderie I had seen between them since they walked in.

"All of those factors are important. I just don't know *how* important yet," I clarified.

At this point, I didn't know if the money required to keep the business open and give the online store a shot would violate or cross a money guardrail, and I also didn't know where their time guardrail was—how long would they want to keep trying until they had to call it quits?

"So," I said. "Let's start by mapping out your collective best-case scenario."

They both agreed by not protesting. I took that as a sign

to continue. I had already run the numbers for them but wanted to suss out what each of their best-case scenarios was and where they saw their time and money guardrails.

I stood up and drew a big line down the middle of my boardroom whiteboard. I wrote *Anne* at the top left and *John* at the top right.

"John." I turned to him. "If the business were to close, what needs to happen before that day in order for you to have no regrets?"

He shifted in his chair. "I guess I'd need to launch the online retail site in earnest so I could see for myself that an online store really won't change things for us."

"What do you mean by that?" I asked.

"I'd need to give it a chance. I really think it's the missing piece. I think it could add passive retirement income. Not only allowing us to break even at the store but making us money again." He looked at Anne. "It's the reason we are failing. We've never even tried."

Anne didn't say anything.

"What does trying look like?" I asked.

"Investing the $40,000 to create the website and market it. Then give it some time," he said.

"How much time?" I pressed.

He sat back in his chair and looked at the ceiling while he thought. This was a totally different side of him. He was in the zone, loving the growth-mindset planning.

"Three years?" he said.

"We can't—" Anne interrupted and he threw his hands up in frustration.

I held up a hand, a signal to let him finish.

"Since time is a constraint for us all," I said, "let me ask the question this way: What's the least amount of time you'd need to let the online store run in order to have no regrets?"

He thought about this for a moment. "At least a year," John said. "Every season. In fact, I'd say 15 months. When our lease is up."

Anne waited a beat before speaking. "We won't survive that long," she said, solemnly. "There's only $25,000 left to spend on the line of credit. We aren't breaking even as is, and if you add in this loan, that's another $1,800 a month to repay. If revenues don't increase, we're out of operating cash-flow within 8 months. We'd either start defaulting on loans or borrowing more, which would put us at risk of bankruptcy. At that point we'd have to start using our own money to pay our corporate lease and payroll."

She was entirely correct. They would be completely out of money in 8 months if they didn't start breaking even.

"Okay, so you have to be breaking even within 8 months." I wrote *8 months* on the board in the middle. "And there'd have to be absolutely no signs of growth. The store would still be losing money." I wrote *Operating loss* on the board.

John piped up. "If we can't get the store breaking even in 8 months, with all our media, advertising, and this digital marketing consultant, then I don't know what it will take to break even. I'm well aware that it takes time to build a new division in any business, but I'm not a stupid man. I don't want to go down in flames."

"I hear you," I said.

I turned to Anne. "What's your best-case scenario here?"

She laughed. "We win the lottery so John can keep the business open, I can retire, and we don't go into debt."

"Interesting," I said. "So, if money wasn't an issue, keeping the business open would be best-case scenario for you?"

"As long as I don't have to work there and it's not costing us anything personally." She shrugged. "It still makes John happy. Plus, he wouldn't be moping around the house all day." She laughed nervously and looked over at him.

"So if you don't win the lottery and the business stays open, what needs to happen for you to have no regrets?" I pressed.

"Oh, I see what you're doing," she said. "It's not that I *want* it to close for the sake of closing—I have loved this business—I just don't want us to be worse off than we are now. I don't have any regrets. And, I guess, I don't want to create any."

"I hear that," I said. "So let me rephrase. What needs to happen for you to avoid *creating* regrets?"

"Well, if the business stays open, I'd have regret if we started putting in any personal money, even a dollar. Or if we ended up with the business in bankruptcy, and everything we built over the years ended in such a disappointing way."

**Money guardrail 1:** No personal money spent
**Money guardrail 2:** No bankruptcy

I was just wondering if there were any time guardrails when Anne answered the question for me.

She sighed. "I also think I need an end date."

"Can you be more specific?" I asked.

"I don't need to quit tomorrow. But I need to know that—win, lose, or draw—I'm out soon. I'm so tired." She looked at John, tears in her eyes. "Our marriage has become a constant battleground over this thing. I'm so done talking about it. I don't care if you keep it open as long as it doesn't hurt us financially and as long as I know I can leave without you resenting me."

John looked down. "I don't resent you," he said gently.

"You will if I quit and you see me as the reason the business had to close. Or if you think I don't have faith in you. I don't want to plunge the business into more debt this close to retirement. I also don't want to make it hard for you to succeed. I just need an end date, and I need to know that everything we've worked so hard for won't be lost."

They were silent for a moment. It was a good moment.

"Can you answer this for me, Anne?"

She looked at me.

"Finish this sentence: *If I cannot quit by X date, I'll have regret.*"

She thought about it. "If we come here next year and I'm still working, I'll have regret."

"Even if the online store is a huge success?" John asked.

"Yes, because if it's a huge success, you can hire someone to replace me and I can finally stop working without feeling guilty."

**Time guardrail 1:** 12 months until Anne stops working

"How much would it cost to replace you at the business?" I asked.

They looked at each other.

"$50,000 a year?" Anne asked John.

"Yeah, probably," he said. "For bookkeeping, inventory tracking, and store management."

"Great," I said and then turned to John. "My take on your combined best-case scenario is that the business stays open and you're able to invest $40,000 for a digital marketing consultant and a new website to get online sales going. After 8 months, the store is not only breaking even but you're able to hire someone for $50,000 a year to replace Anne. Anne leaves before 12 months is up."

He thought about it for a moment before responding.

"Well, I plan to grow *much* more than that. But, yes, that's my best-case scenario for this exercise."

I went back to Anne. "In order to avoid creating regret, not as much as $1 can transfer from the household bank accounts to the business. And you need to know the business could support enough money to replace you within 12 months."

"Plus no bankruptcy," she added.

"No bankruptcy," I said.

I wrote the following on the board:

## BEST-CASE SCENARIO:

- Store stays open
- Anne stops working after 1 year
- Online store launches

"So this is your joint plan. Your collective best-case scenario with some guardrails."

"Guardrails?" Anne asked, raising her brow.

"Time and money guardrails. You have both. The events that will force you to stop trying to reach your collective best-case scenario. When you have no choice but to call it quits."

Then I wrote the following:

**Time guardrail:** 12 months until Anne stops working

"If the online store is up and running, you have a marketing consultant, and orders are coming in but you can't afford to replace Anne after 12 months, you call it quits. Agreed?" I asked.

They both nodded.

**Money guardrail 1:** No personal money spent to support the business

"If you're in a situation where you can't make ends meet and the only way would be to start putting personal retirement money in, you call it quits. Everyone aligned on that?" I asked.

They both nodded.

**Money guardrail 2:** No bankruptcy threat

"You said that the business would have to go bankrupt if debt climbed over $135,000. So if corporate debt threatens to go over $135,000, you call it. Agreed?"

They did.

"If any of these things happen, they are your agreed-upon limits. Lines in the sand that you both accept. You're going to try to make the business work. You'll invest the $40,000 to see if the business can break even within 8 months and support someone to replace Anne in 12 months."

They were nodding along with me.

"If this is what you do, one of two things will happen: Either the online shop turns things around and the store stays open profitably, which is John's dream, and Anne gets to retire without any regrets. Or you try everything you safely could but nothing changes. Then the store closes but John has no regrets or resentment and your personal finances are still intact."

They both looked at the board for some time.

Anne spoke first. "It feels like a million decisions have been narrowed down to one plan of action."

"Yes," I said. "And it's a plan that gives you both a chance at a best-case scenario before you have to make the hard decision to stop."

"So what's next?" John asked.

"Well, that depends. If everything works out, I'll see you for some retirement planning in a year."

"And if it doesn't?" Anne asked with an eyebrow raised.

I took a big breath and let it out. "If it doesn't, come and see me when you hit one of your guardrails. Time or money."

"What happens then?" John asked.

"It will be time to make a hard choice," I said.

As they left, I was excited and nervous for them. The stakes were high—both emotionally and financially—and so much still hung in the balance.

When you hit one of your guardrails, that's that. Or at least that *should* be that. Remember that when you put those guardrails into place, you did it for a reason. They made you feel safe at the time. Pushing beyond them felt irresponsible or scary or unsafe. When you put those guardrails in place, the entire point was to let you know when you've reached the point when continuing will lead to regret. The point where the cost no longer outweighs the benefit.

If you want to keep pushing beyond your time or financial guardrail, then it wasn't really a guardrail in the first place. It was a pivot point. A point when you needed to make big trade-offs or sacrifices to allot more money and time than initially anticipated to keep trying for your best-case scenario. But that's different.

Hitting a pivot point isn't the point of no return. It's simply the point where you need to adjust your other plans in order to keep going.

If you have imposed time or money guardrails, it's murkier. You'll know if you've hit a pivot point versus a guardrail because you may start negotiating: *Maybe just a bit longer* or *Maybe a bit more money.*

If you're in a position to ask these questions, then you have options. You haven't reached the point of no return yet. You still have levers you can pull to keep trying to achieve your best-case scenario.

True time or money guardrails provide clarity and even relief. There are no more levers. There are no more options. It's time.

When you hit those guardrails, you'll need to think back to when you first laid them out. You established guardrails by asking yourself how far you'd go until you would have regret. That's what's at stake.

The only good thing about hitting a guardrail is that at least there is no more wondering. You know, once and for all, that the best-case scenario is not going to play out. There is an odd relief in that. Wondering and waffling can be stressful.

Eight months after our initial meeting, John and Anne were back in my office. They were barely speaking. John could hardly look at either of us. It was tense.

"So, John, I'll start with you. How are you feeling about everything?" I asked gently.

"How do you think?" he asked with a clenched jaw.

"I don't know, actually. That's why I'm asking."

"I suppose you could say I'm a bit disappointed." His voice dripped sarcasm.

Slowly the story unfolded. Over the last 8 months, John and Anne had worked their butts off. Not only on the day-to-day business, but they had also invested the $40,000 in a digital marketing manager and launched a beautiful online retail shop. The only problem? Sales were underwhelming.

## THE FACTS:

- The business line of credit went from $75,000 to $85,000 owing.
- There had been moderate online retail sales but not enough to break even.
- Online advertisements had not proven profitable for them.
- They had used the entire $40,000 business investment loan.

It wasn't looking good. They hadn't reached a time or money guardrail yet, but they were very close. If you recall, their guardrails looked like this:

**Time guardrail:** 12 months until Anne stops working (4 months away)
**Money guardrail:** No personal money spent (still hadn't)
**Money guardrail:** No bankruptcy (not yet)

While they hadn't put any personal money into the business and their household income remained constant, there was only $10,000 left to borrow. Eight months in and they were almost completely tapped.

"I'm so sorry," I offered. "I know this isn't the way either of you wanted this to pan out. This must be heartbreaking."

Anne spoke first. "It is. I just don't think that we are going to get online sales up to a point where we are breaking even or can hire my replacement in 4 months. At this point, that feels like a bit of a pipe dream."

"John, what do you think?" I asked.

He didn't respond right away. He looked away with his hand over his mouth. After a moment, he sighed. "I think we should keep going. We have all the right things in place. We just need more time."

Anne shifted and pressed her lips together before speaking. "John, we don't have any more time. There's no more money. I thought we agreed on this."

He sat forward. "Yes, but sales are always slow in the beginning of a new business line. You know that. I think you're being too short-sighted. The site is good and there *are* sales. We just have to keep marketing."

They both looked at me. Anne and John had clearly reached a *crossroads crisis* and now had to make hard decisions—decisions that wouldn't leave them feeling happy either way. I worried they thought I was going to pick sides, but that's not what I do. Any decisions made had to be their own.

"With only $10,000 left on the business line of credit, we'll be out of working capital in a couple of months," Anne said.

"We could extend the line of credit," John said. "We've been good customers with the bank. We could buy more time."

"But that was one of our hard lines in the sand!" Anne said.

"No, bankruptcy is the point of no return," John said. "This isn't going to bankrupt us. We'd need to borrow $50,000 to hit that point. I'm suggesting another $15,000."

He was right. I pulled their file up on screen and let them read it.

**Time guardrail:** 12 months until Anne stops working
**Money guardrail:** No personal money spent
**Money guardrail:** No bankruptcy

John shook his head. "These are silly. To run an entire business based on hopes from a few months ago."

"At the time," I said, "you both agreed that these were more than hopes. You both agreed that these were things that needed to happen to ensure you both have no regrets." I turned to Anne. "Do you think an increase to the line of credit is up for debate? Do you think it's a pivot point, not a money guardrail?"

"That depends," she said and looked at John. "How much more time do you think you need?"

"Another year," he said. "At least. To really give it a shot. You can quit, I'll hire someone."

She shook her head slowly. "Sweetie, unless sales take off in a major way tomorrow, we'd need to borrow at least another $50,000 to replace me. Even if we liquidated everything, at that level of debt, the business would have to go bankrupt."

He didn't say anything. He just stared at the table, flicking his pen.

Anne looked at me. "Which is why I can't leave. Not even in 4 months. We can't afford for me to leave. It's not a real time guardrail at all."

They both sat in silence.

Finally, John spoke. "We could earn so much more than we are now. With online sales, I wouldn't have to have retail space anymore. The lease is almost up. Then all of the money would go to us. It's the next evolution. But it takes time to market. You know this!" He was getting agitated again.

"John," she said calmly. "We are too old to roll the dice again. We don't have enough time or money. We are almost at the end of the line here. We agreed on this. We had a plan."

He shook his head. "There is a viable business model here, Anne. There is. It just needs more time. A few more years until online sales catch on in a big way."

"We don't have a few more years," she said. Her voice cracked. "Even if I stay on, unless sales suddenly take off tomorrow, we've got 6 months tops until we are completely out of money and everything we've worked for ends in bankruptcy. I don't want that for you. For us."

John was up and pacing now. He looked at me. "So what you're saying is we stay open, my wife hates me and her life, and we have less than 1 year to get an entire online sales division off the ground otherwise we go bankrupt and my wife still hates me."

Anne shook her head. "John, come—"

John interrupted her. "Or we close now, *she's* happy, and I'm left with nothing. No store, no future cash-flow opportunities. Nothing."

I kept quiet.

"This is so pathetic," he said. "To see my entire life's work laid out in two shit choices."

"John," I said gently. "What do you think the cost of doing nothing is at this point?"

"I don't even know," he said.

"I suppose doing nothing would be worse," Anne offered. "John never gets to build the online store in the way he wants to, I keep working and never get to leave, and we still wind up with $150,000 debt. We still wind up bankrupt."

"So doing nothing isn't a choice," I stated.

"No," she said.

I saw John shake his head.

"I know this is hard," I said. "It's good that you already have hard lines in place. At some point, it will become unsafe to proceed any further. But perhaps Anne leaving at 12 months isn't a real time guardrail. Perhaps it's only a pivot point. A point where you change other life plans in order to carry on," I offered.

I crossed out *Anne leaving the business in 12 months* on the screen.

"So really, these are the only guardrails left."

~~Time Guardrail~~ **Pivot point:** 12 months until Anne stops working
**Money guardrail:** No personal money spent
**Money guardrail:** No bankruptcy

"Now we know that $135,000 of business debt is the maximum you can afford without dipping into your personal finances. That becomes the line in the sand between being able to close and breakeven versus bankruptcy.

"That's only $10,000 away, Shannon," Anne said. "We are already at an impasse."

"You are," I agreed. "It's no longer hypothetical. It's right around the corner. But everything that is within your control is known at this point. You have to ask yourselves: Can you emotionally afford to keep the store open for the next year to try to build a potential future revenue stream? Or can you emotionally afford to close the store and walk away?"

"You know what?" John said, collecting his papers, "I don't need this. Thank you very much for your time." He looked at Anne. "I'll walk home." And with that, he got up and left the office. It was the first time that had happened in over a decade. I've never forgotten it.

"I'm so sorry," Anne said, welling up. "He's not actually an asshole, I promise."

"I don't think he's an asshole at all," I said. And I meant it. "He's hurt and angry. This is an extremely difficult situation. This business has been your whole life. It's his identity, it's who he is. After all the hard work, to feel like no matter what you choose, you don't get to be happy . . . it's a tough pill to swallow."

My heart broke for him. For Anne too.

"You're right. The business has been everything to him. His social life, passion, hobby—everything. I honestly think he will be happier without it one day, but he doesn't even see that as a possibility because he's so angry."

"At who?" I asked.

"The world. Anytime he reads something about retail shops closing, or the death of retail, his whole mood just changes. He spent all Christmas day in his office brooding because on Christmas Eve we heard on the radio that online sales were at record highs this year. He missed out on all the joy. He's obsessed."

"That must be hard for everyone."

"It's not ending how he wants it to end." She grabbed a tissue and dabbed tears at the side of her eyes. "It was supposed to be this legacy. We had dreams of our kids taking it over." She laughed. "They want nothing to do with it, which he takes as a personal offence."

"It's interesting that you're more at peace with letting it go than he is, given that you've both owned it for 25 years."

She dabbed away more tears. "That's because I left my career to help him. I mean, we had some great memories, but it was always his baby. His dream. Now I want a life of my own, but I feel trapped."

"That's the thing about hard decisions. They are hard for a reason. All you can do now is focus on your values, pivot if you can, and call it quits when you need to so you don't regret anything."

"So, ultimately, I need to ask myself if John's future happiness has a higher value than my need for peace and quiet."

"Or John needs to choose whether his value of success ranks higher than your future peace of mind."

She laughed. "No big deal, right?"

I laughed with her. "Life is messy. But I think it would be boring without all the mess. The mess means high stakes.

High stakes mean you were really living."

We hugged and I wished her luck. When she left, it didn't have that celebratory vibe that usually happens. I felt as sad as Anne did. So much still had to unfold.

Six months later, Anne, and only Anne, was back to check in.

"He may come," she said as she sat down. "He may not."

"I'm okay with that as long as both of you are too."

"We're good," she confirmed.

"So where are we at? Tell me everything."

She took a deep breath and started in. "At the start, we carried on as if our second meeting had never happened. Doing nothing. No decision made. We barely spoke about it, actually."

"Okay," I said, with a bit of trepidation.

"So a month went by. We didn't break even again and the online sales were dismal. Not even $1,000. I feel like that was a breaking point for John. He couldn't pretend that it wasn't happening. Our lease was also coming up, which was the catalyst for us to actually sit down and talk. We were almost $135,000 in debt by then, and we were both aligned that we didn't want to go bankrupt. That money guardrail we talked about was still in place."

"So?"

She took a deep breath. "So we closed the store."

I nodded and remained silent.

"We had a fire sale, and now we are having the lawyers and accountants do their thing." She let out a long sigh.

"How do you feel?"

"Sad and relieved. A decision has finally been made. No more wondering. No more what-ifs. No more fighting. But it is sad. It was a part of me too. It's the end of an era."

"It really is," I said. "Do you have any regrets?"

She thought about it. "I really do think John is brilliant. I think if we had started the online store 5 years ago, we could have had that income stream and passive income in retirement he dreamed of. We were just too late to the game, and we are too old to risk it all now. I think we both just regret that we didn't think about it sooner and avoided this mess altogether."

"Shoulda, woulda, coulda."

"Exactly."

"Any regrets about your decisions given how it actually played out?"

She smiled. "No. I'm really glad I didn't just walk away when we hit that time guardrail, or pivot point, I guess. Though, I wanted to many times. I'm glad we made the time guardrail a pivot point. I choose to give it one last chance."

"How'd that feel?" I asked.

"I thought leaving at the original 12-month mark was a hard line for me, but when I got there, it wasn't as important as I thought. I just had to pivot my own expectations. I know we could have had a little bit more of a nest egg if we had closed a year ago, when we first came in and not spent the $40,000 on the online store and consultant, but honestly, his happiness is important for my peace of mind. His happiness makes me feel . . . content."

"And how's John?" I asked.

"He's good, actually," she said.

I felt an instant rush of relief. I didn't realize I had been holding my shoulders up around my ears. "I'm glad."

"Having the money guardrail, the $135,000 debt marker, was invaluable for us both. It allowed me to relax and not freak out over every little thing while we were spending money to get the online sales up because I knew we were still going to be okay as long as we didn't have more than $135,000 of debt. But truly, it took the emotion out of the choice to close when we reached it. I said, 'John, we have $5,000 left to borrow until we are completely insolvent. I don't want our legacy to end like this.' And that really resonated with him. It really helped him see that it was time to act. That time was up."

I nodded. "Does he have any regrets?"

"Same as mine. Wishing we had started the online store years and years ago instead of cramming it into the last year here. But he is glad that we at least tried."

"Why isn't he here today?" I asked, not sure I wanted to know the answer.

"It's still pretty fresh for him. His exact words were 'What's the point in hashing it out? What's done is done.'"

I nodded. He wasn't wrong.

"He will be okay. We are telling friends and our entrepreneur community that we planned it this way. That online sales just wasn't our thing and that our landlord wanted a ridiculous amount of money to sign back on. That part is true, actually. No one is questioning us. Everyone totally understands. It's allowed us to close gracefully. Which is important to us both."

"What's his mood like on a daily basis?" I asked.

"Some days are nostalgic or a bit sad, but he doesn't have the same rage or temper that he had near the end there. I feel like I'm seeing John again."

"I'm happy for you both," I said. "So what's next?"

"I'm going to spend time with the kids and I want to take a trip soon. John, well, he will never not work. I'm sure he's already starting another business. Probably a business to put online retailers out of business."

I laughed. "Entrepreneurship can be addictive," I said.

"It sure can be."

"One last question."

She looked up.

"Are you proud of your decisions and do you think John is too?"

She thought about this for some time.

"Yes," she said at last. "I know I am, even though we were in more debt than I would like and we didn't really walk away with any business assets, I'm proud of the fact that I gave it one last go. Not only for John, but also for the store and everything we built together. I'm proud that we came together, in the end, to make the decision as a team. As for John, he's actually told me that he is proud."

"Really?" I asked.

"Yes. He's proud of himself for trying, for not going down without a fight and that when it was over, he was smart enough to end it before it ended him. To know when to call it quits and finish on his terms. He's proud of how it ended.

He really is."

"That's great to hear."

"You really did help us," she said.

"I'm so glad and I hope John feels the same way."

"He does," she assured me. "He's just old."

We laughed.

"And stubborn," she added.

When you reach your guardrail—be it time or money—you'll know it. There is no more room for negotiation. There are no more *what-ifs*. The emotional cost of regret or the unsafe position it puts you in far outweigh the potential benefit of continuing to try for your best-case scenario. But that's how you survive it.

If you can look back and know that you tried, that you played the best possible hand you could but were also smart enough to know when to call it, that *is* a win. Even if you don't win the game. Being smart enough to know when to call it is just as important as knowing when to keep trying.

Guardrails need to be in place so you can absolve yourself of anxiety while you're waiting to see if your best-case scenario can play out because you know you're not going to spin out of control. With guardrails in place, you'll know that you're still going to be safe and, because you won't wind up with regret, you'll also be happy in your next normal.

## HOMEWORK: FIND YOUR TIME GUARDRAILS

Here are the steps to create your time guardrails.

**Step 1:** Outline your best-case scenario.

**Step 2:** Imagine you won the lottery and money was no object. Would there still be a point in time when you stopped going after your best-case scenario? When is that point? This is your time guardrail.

**Step 3:** Check in. If you stopped trying to achieve your best-case scenario by your time guardrail, would you have regret? If yes, however long that is becomes your time guardrail. The line in the sand between *go* and *stop*. If not, then proceed to Step 4.

**Step 4:** Final check-in. At what point in time do you need to stop trying to go after your best-case scenario so that you don't regret the amount of time it took to get there?

**Step 5:** Write down the guardrails. Write down the reason something is a guardrail for you. Why is it important for you to stop when you hit this point? Do this now so that you can refer to the guardrails down the road when you potentially hit them and need to remember that you made this choice for a reason.

## HOMEWORK: FIND YOUR MONEY GUARDRAILS
Here are the steps to create your money guardrails.

**Step 1:** Outline your best-case scenario.

**Step 2:** Outline your worst-case scenario.

**Step 3:** Look for financial outcomes that scare you in your worst-case scenario. They likely scare you for a reason. They make you feel unsafe or you're worried you'll regret them.

**Step 4:** Check in. Ask yourself the hard questions. Use an extreme measure like *Would I go bankrupt in pursuit of my best-case scenario?* or *How much debt would I go in to achieve my best-case scenario?* or *How much of my savings would I spend to reach my best-case scenario?*

**Step 5:** Check in. Look for regret. If any of the financial outcomes in Step 4 happened, would you have regret? If yes, then this becomes your money guardrail–the line between spending without regret and spending so much that you'd have regret.

**Step 6:** Write down your money guardrails. Include the reason this is a guardrail for you. Why is it important for you to stop when you hit this point? Do this now so that you can refer to your reasons when you potentially hit your guardrail and need to remember that you made this choice for a reason.

# CHAPTER 10:

## Dealing with 100% Uncertainty

So far, we've talked about situations where we can find some measure of certainty, no matter how small, that enables us to make micro goals and mini timelines, and put pivots and guardrails in place to help us get to the other side of a crisis. But sometimes, no matter what you've done or how carefully you've planned, there will be situations where the only certainty is 100% uncertainty. A medical condition or rare illness, for example, where traditional treatment here offers a degree of success but no guarantee and an experimental treatment abroad offers slightly more success but still with no guarantee. One is covered by insurance, the other will take almost all of your savings. Which do you choose when all you want is hope, but there are no guarantees either way?

Situations with absolutely no short-term predictability, where it's impossible to set pivot points and time or money guardrails, mean the Decision Crisis Playbook can't work in the traditional way. When facing this kind of dilemma, the only path to no-regret decisions is to focus on gathering helpful information that upholds your deciding values and to block out unhelpful information.

*Helpful information* comes from trusted resources, ones that help you feel like you're making the right choices while still upholding your deciding values. *Unhelpful information* is the kind that tempts you to make decisions that don't uphold your deciding values, which ultimately causes anxiety, makes you waffle on your plan, and leads to self-doubt.

When all you have is 100% uncertainty in the outcome, put your faith in trusted resources and block out the information that makes you doubt yourself.

## MEET KAI
AGE: 42
RELATIONSHIP STATUS: Dating
KIDS: None

I met Kai for the first time a few years ago. Kai had been diagnosed with multiple sclerosis 6 months previously and was looking for advice on how to navigate their finances in the face of such uncertainty.

"So yeah," they said after laying out everything that had happened in the 6 months prior to our meeting. "That's where I'm at."

I let out a big breath. "That's a lot."

"It is," they said, eyes downcast, fingertips drumming soundlessly on my desk.

I could see the effort to remain calm, reasonable, the pillar of strength they had always been. The one who cared for others, planned responsibly, and knew exactly which direction the future was going—a future that was no more certain than a roll of the dice, a future they had never seen coming.

The good news was that Kai was making great money as a TV producer. A few years after their father passed away, Kai's sister wanted their elderly mother to live with either herself or Kai. Since neither of them wanted Mom to live alone, Kai moved her into their previously rented basement apartment.

"My mother's not sick," Kai said. "But we all decided she shouldn't live alone any longer. My mom and dad are first-generation immigrants. They rented their whole lives so she didn't have a house to sell and downsize. All my parents' savings went to support me and my sister. We both graduated without student debt, and our parents also helped us buy our first homes. We were so lucky. We *are* so lucky."

I nodded.

"My sister lives in Edmonton," Kai continued. "So Mom moved in with me. It's been good. She's got her space, I've got mine." A smile twitched at the corners of their mouth.

"My mom likes my new partner, which is amazing. The two of them get along so well that we all started having dinner together on Sundays."

"Sounds like your partner is one of the good ones."

"His name is Nils. He's one of the best." Kai lowered their eyes again and stopped smiling. "Honestly, I'm surprised he hasn't jumped and run since my diagnosis. I couldn't ask for more from either him or my mom. I mean, Nils was doing fine before we met, but financially my mom would be in trouble without me. She has nothing—just her government pensions—so it's up to my sister and me to provide for her. We always had a plan for what to do if *Mom* got sick." Kai shrugged and looked out the window. "But we didn't have a plan to cover what would happen if I got sick and couldn't work."

"How can I help?" I asked.

They took another deep breath, clearly determined to remain calm. "My job is really intense. Very high stress sometimes, which isn't great for my health, putting me in a really hard position. If I need to leave work, or earn less by working less, it not only impacts my personal financial security, it also impacts my mom's. And the future Nils and I had just started planning." Those fingers started drumming again. "We don't know when, but we all know that at some point in the future, hopefully the far-away future, I'll need to make some really tough decisions."

"What decisions are those?" I asked.

Kai said nothing for a moment, then nodded once and started in. "Well, for starters, all my money is in the house.

I'd probably have to sell it if I couldn't work. I do have long-term disability insurance, but it wouldn't pay enough each month to cover the cost of the house and living expenses." The words were coming faster and faster, as though saying them out loud had opened a gate that had been closed for too long. "I have savings, but I'm only 42 and the disability policy will only pay out until I'm 65. Essentially, I will need to sell the house for money if I have to leave my job, or maybe even for mobility reasons before that. Sell it, move to a bungalow. It all depends on my health."

I nodded and turned to the whiteboard and wrote *When to sell house*. "I'm gathering that the timeline on this is anywhere from tomorrow to never," I said.

Kai shrugged. "Exactly. I have to know when to pull the trigger. Do I sell now, before things are bad? Just in case? Do I wait it out? It's hard to know and impossible to answer all the questions that my family and Nils aren't asking." They looked at me. "You know what I mean?"

"I do," I said and set down the marker. "What's your best-case scenario right now?"

"Best case is that I can keep working without the diagnosis negatively impacting my health, that I can still earn enough money to support myself and my mother. And that Nils keeps believing that we have some kind of future, despite all of this."

"Sounds like *Family* and *Health* are your core values—the ones you want to honour the most in this decision on when to sell the house."

"Absolutely."

"Do you want those to be your deciding values through-out this process?"

They nodded so I wrote that down.

"Now we need to think about your worst-case scenario."

"I feel like there are two."

"Let me have them."

"First would be my health deteriorating quickly. Having to leave work, sell the . . ." They paused and tilted their head to the side. "Well, actually, I'm not sure."

"What are you not sure about?"

"Obviously I don't want my health to deteriorate quickly but, to be honest, that's not what I'm losing sleep over right now. Which sounds crazy."

"What are you losing sleep over?" I asked.

"I think I'm afraid of making a bad decision. It's like, if I'm sick and need to stop working, there's no choice but to sell the house for whatever price it's worth. I wouldn't have any regrets, even if I sold at a loss because it would be totally out of my hands and have to happen. My actual worry is that I sell the house out of panic right now and miss out on future growth over the next 20 years, which could make or break my mom and mine's financial situation down the road. It wouldn't be good for any of us."

"What's important about 20 years?" I asked.

"I don't know. I just didn't see myself downsizing until my 60s. If I sold before 20 years, it would only be because my health was bad."

"I understand."

"My sister keeps pressuring me to sell, sell, sell *right now* because housing prices have skyrocketed. I know her heart is in the right place, but I've started avoiding her phone calls. I guess I'm also afraid she's right. That I'd be in trouble if housing prices go down and I have to sell at a bad time. Bird in the hand, you know."

"That's hard to predict."

"Totally."

"What's the other big decisions you have to make?" I asked.

"Whether to quit my job."

I nodded.

"So it's very black and white. If I'm healthy, I want to stay in the house. I want to keep believing in the future. If I'm not, I need to be realistic and move. There's no world where I can live in the house if I'm not earning money or if my mobility goes. There's not a lot of middle ground for me."

"Normally I'd want us to set some pivot points, a sort of red-flag system that outlines when your other life plans need to change in order to keep chasing your best-case scenario. For example, other things you'd have to give up before you sold the house. But it doesn't really feel like we can do that here."

"What do you mean?"

"An example of a pivot point could be that if your health starts to be impacted and you have to leave work, maybe you scale back, not leave work entirely so you can keep the house for 20 years. Or perhaps you use some savings. Essentially, give up other life plans and pull resources toward the main goal of staying in the house. But as you say, those aren't really options."

They gave a short laugh. "Scaling back at work isn't an option. It's stressful no matter what. If I'm scaling back, it's because my health is not good and so I'd have to remove all work at that point. Also, I've spoken to my employer. Part time isn't an option because half income would be the same as disability and more dangerous to my health."

"There's not really a middle ground, or compromise point."

They started drumming again. "None at all."

"So no pivot points." I sat back in my chair. "I feel like it's also hard to set any money or time guardrails—a certain point in time or a certain amount of money that would dictate when you sold, no matter what."

Kai's eyes stayed focused on their fingers. "Like, when would I sell the house even if I was healthy before age 60?"

"Yes."

"If I'm healthy, I want to keep the house forever. I love my house."

"You mentioned that your sister wants you to sell and that stresses you out."

"It does. That's the creeping anxiety that keeps me up at night. Like holding on to the house until I get sick will come back to haunt me."

I thought for a moment. "Sometimes in the financial world, when it comes to investing, you set an upper price limit on a stock. For example, before I invest, I make the decision that if a stock I purchase for $10 goes to $50, I'll sell. No matter what, even if I think the stock may continue to rise. Up front, I decide that a $40 profit is enough money. When I sell, I'll have that money in the bank and be happy with the profit. Those limits help take emotions out of trading decisions. It's predetermined. I wonder if there's a similar perspective we could take with the house? Is there a predetermined price that it could either rise to or fall to that would prompt you to sell?"

They thought about this but didn't say anything.

"This could be a money guardrail," I said. "A financial point where you'd sell no matter what was happening to avoid regret later on."

"I mean, I think I'd like to live in the house forever. So, truly, I'd only sell if I needed money. I'm prepared to do that after 20 years and I expect to. But the only reason I'd sell is if I had to."

"When to sell or not to sell."

"That *is* the question."

Our laughter was genuine, breaking the tension that these intense discussions often create. Then I went back to the whiteboard.

"So we have neither pivot points nor true time or money guardrails. Essentially, whenever your health goes down, you'll sell, leaving us with no predictability whatsoever."

They leaned back in the chair. "Not fun."

"Definitely not," I agreed. "But I believe that we can still find a way to avoid regret and escape your fear of making a bad decision when you do, if you ever do, decide to sell. First of all, how often do you think you'll have to make this choice? Or assess the situation?"

"Um, daily? I think that's why I'm so stressed out. I feel like I never get a break from this waffling."

"That sounds intense."

"It is. I get all these texts from my sister or hear more news about housing prices and I am overwhelmed with guilt, like I need to reconvince myself to stay. It's a constant source of stress."

"I can see that. No offence to your sister, or the media, but those don't feel like helpful resources for this decision at the moment."

"You're right. My sister means well, but it's not helpful."

"What you need is a different resource list. A list of people or resources who *can* help you navigate this decision and uphold your deciding values, and then you can block out unhelpful information. Imagine there were no texts from your sister and no media coverage on housing prices. How would you know when to sell?"

"I guess when my doctor told me that my symptoms are progressing."

I wrote *Doctors* in a *Helpful Information* list.

"What else?"

"I need to know that the housing market is relatively stable. I don't intend to sell, but I'd like to make sure that I'm not in a sinking ship."

"Who can help with that information?"

"I guess my realtor? He's my pal and I trust him."

"What's his current take?"

"Hold for life," they said with a wide smile.

I wrote *Real estate check-in* on the list.

"Anything else?"

They thought for a moment. "I believe my mental health is important here."

"That checks out."

Kai laughed. "My doctor can help with the physical side of my health but juggling all of this is a lot. So even though my physical health might be fine, if my mental health isn't fine, maybe I need to consider selling to stop the endless waffling and finally land."

"What information do you need to ensure your mental health remains a priority?"

"My therapist needs to see no red flags. That will help me gauge whether the goal of holding on to the house is taking a toll on my mental health."

I wrote that down and then read the list aloud.

"Okay, here is the information that is helpful to keep your health a priority while also pursuing the goal of keeping your house."

- Doctor gives physical go-ahead to keep working
- Therapist raises no red flags
- No real-estate red flags

They read the list and agreed. "I feel like this is very helpful."

"Good!" I laughed. "Tell me why?"

"First and foremost, my physical health is honoured, which is the most important to me. But having my mental health be a priority as well as ensuring I'm not being financially irresponsible feels reassuring. If I'm checking in with these people, then I won't have to worry about having regrets." They paused. "It's easier to blame other people if it doesn't work out." They laughed then turned serious again. "I'm joking, but also kind of not. It's hard shouldering this massive decision all on my own."

"It must be. That's why it's good to share the load." I turned back to the list. "Now we need to think about the kind of information that is *not* helpful, the type that makes you doubt yourself and waffle."

"Like my sister's texts?"

"For this specific situation, I think yes. Usually when we make choices, other people always have well-meaning tips, advice, and opinions or we read unhelpful information elsewhere."

"Okay," they said and paused. "Unhelpful information." They cracked their knuckles, like they were about to go into a boxing match. "This will be fun."

I wasn't surprised at the first.

"I have to talk to my sister and ask her to stop texting me about selling."

I wrote down *Real-estate advice from others (except chosen realtor).*

"And constant internet housing coverage," they added. "I have to mute it, unsubscribe to newsletters and certain message boards, so I don't get sucked in by click-bait headlines and comments from people I have never even met."

"Yes, I've been doing this a long time. I've never seen 'opinions from the internet' as helpful information for people."

We laughed together.

"The internet is a cesspool."

"It most definitely can be," I agreed.

I added *Housing price hoopla* to the list.

"Oh," Kai said, clearly warming up more and more to making this list. "And ignoring medical suggestions from social media or friends that go against what my doctor is saying regarding my diagnosis and my treatments. It's not that I don't believe in other methods, but I'm not there yet. I have faith in my doctor and our plan, I'm meditating, I've changed my lifestyle, I'm making self-care a priority, I'm doing all the things. So when someone says, *Have you tried this?* I just want to tell them to shut up."

I nodded and translated that to *Try this/that.*

"Anything else?"

"I think that's it."

I put the marker down. "Can I ask a potentially loaded question?"

"Sure."

"You haven't mentioned Nils."

They shrugged. "I don't want to put him anywhere. I still can't believe how supportive he's been, but what will happen if I get worse? I can't put pressure on him."

"I understand," I said gently. "So let's look at ways you can you ensure that you avoid these types of unhelpful information resources."

"I am really looking forward to muting people that are triggering on social media. Or maybe get off social media entirely. It feels extreme, but I'm always so stressed out after being on it. Maybe I mute almost everyone and only follow cat memes and astrology profiles."

"That's almost entirely my internet feed too." We both smiled, then I added, "And what about media real-estate coverage?"

"*Ugh,* I know. I think I just have to literally turn off the radio when that subject comes on. I also want to unsubscribe from a few realtor profiles I've set up. I did this so I could monitor housing prices, but again, it's just making me more stressed out."

We turned back to the final lists.

## HELPFUL INFORMATION SOURCES NEEDED TO UPHOLD DECIDING VALUES:
- Doctor gives physical go-ahead
- Therapist raises no red flags
- No real-estate red flags

## UNHELPFUL INFORMATION SOURCES:
- Sister's texts
- Real-estate news
- Social media break

Kai nodded. "This feels really helpful."

"I'm glad," I said. "What do you find most helpful about it?"

"The decision to sell the house is filled with anxiety. So many *what-ifs.* But this makes it feel like there's at least a plan, like one of those magazine decision quizzes." They put on a fake voice, "Did your doctor give you the go-ahead? Yes or no. If yes, click here. Like a playbook."

I smiled to myself. "That's exactly what this is. A Decision Crisis Playbook. A tool that's great for decision-making when you're in a situation where you can't predict or pivot anything."

"A mini decision tree."

"Decorated with good information."

We smiled.

I gestured to the list again. "Everything in those three questions is all the information you need in order to make your decision for now. Everything else is noise. Block it out."

"I love it," they said. "Here's information that matters, here's what doesn't. Decide based on these, block everything else out. It feels black and white in a world where everything is grey."

And that was the goal.

By using helpful information and avoiding unhelpful information, you're putting your faith in trusted information sources.

If you're in a situation where the future is 100% unpredictable and you have to make high-stakes decisions without any pivot plans or guardrails, the best thing to do is to isolate your deciding values. Figure out the helpful information that upholds those values and ignore information that makes you fall into panic mode. This helps you feel like you have a plan and some control when there is none.

## HOMEWORK: GATHER GOOD INFORMATION

**Step 1:** Prioritize your deciding values.

**Step 2:** Create a timeline that aligns with your decision-making timeline. For example, if you need to make a decision in 2 weeks, the timeline is 2 weeks. If you need to make a decision in 3 months, the timeline is 3 months.

**Step 3:** Make a list of information that gives you clarity and motivates you to make choices that honour your deciding values within your timeline.

**Step 4:** Create a list of how you can get that information or who can give you that information.

## HOMEWORK: AVOID UNPRODUCTIVE INFORMATION

**Step 1:** What information makes you feel anxious, frustrated, or angry? What information conflicts with the information that gives you clarity and motivates you to make choices that honour your deciding values within your timeline?

**Step 2:** What actions can you take to actively avoid exposures to that information during your timeline? For example, you might have to have a tough conversation with someone about the negative information they are imparting to you. Or you may have to get off social media, mute people, or stop going to certain websites.

# PHASE 3:

## Your Next Normal

# CHAPTER 11:

## Embracing Your Next Normal

You made it. You've followed all the steps—focusing on your deciding values, creating micro goals and timelines, putting guardrails in place—and here you are, ready, maybe even excited, for what comes next.

No more stress from waffling. *Do you? Don't you? Will it? Won't it? What if?* All of that is done now. You've made your decision. Congratulations.

Let's take a moment to acknowledge how far you've come in your decision crisis journey. You know how to get out of panic mode and into a growth mindset, even if only for a moment. You've mapped out your decision tree. You know your deciding values. You've assigned any short- or long-term predictability where you can. You know what good information to use and what to avoid. You've mapped out your pivot points. You've set your time and money guardrails to ensure you are safe and happy on the other side of this. The best part? You've made your choice. *Whoa.*

Your choice happened in the messy middle. Now welcome to your next normal. Whether your decision crisis lasted a week or whether it's been a long 5 years, the very act of making it to the end of the decision crisis is huge.

So now what?

What is your next normal? What can you expect? How will you feel? Will you really embrace your decisions without regret?

There is literally nothing for you to do now but take a deep breath in and wait to see what happens next. You know you've packed your parachute the best you can. You've done all the work. You've made the leap and now there's nothing left to do as you fall but trust and wait for the parachute to open at the right time.

If you've made your decision(s), and things work out as you want them to, that's amazing. It means you're going to like your next normal. Your values have been upheld and you have no regrets. It's easy to have no regrets when things work out exactly how you want them to.

As with all big decisions made during difficult times, you may have sacrificed a lot. If you don't end up loving your next normal, it's hard not to have regret for the choices you made, but hindsight is always 20/20.

Imagine you moved from the city to the country. At the time, the decision made financial sense. You've got a deciding value around financial security and the city was too expensive. You've got a core value around adventure and moving to the country gives you that sense of adventure since you're close to nature. But what if, after the move, you're lonely? You love so many aspects about rural life, but you miss your community. You miss the city noise (more than you thought). You're bored. You're just not sure you like this next normal you created. Should you regret your decision?

No!

If you made your decisions following the Decision Crisis Playbook, you shouldn't have regret, no matter how things played out. You made decisions based on your values and the most helpful information you had at the time. If the decision to move to the country truly upheld your deciding values, then it may just take time until those deciding values start to shine through. You may just need more time. Be patient.

If you're not happy about how things played out and you feel pangs of regret, you'll need to find your way back to having no regrets because regret will rob you of any chance you have of enjoying your next normal. Worst of all, it robs you of your confidence to make good decisions in the future.

That's why it's so important not to feel regret. I have seen this time and time again. Regret steals your hope for the future.

In my job, I hear about regrets a lot:

*I should have said yes to that job.*

*I should have gone on that trip.*

*I should have bought that house.*

*I shouldn't have married that person.*

My answer to should/shouldn't is almost always the same: *Maybe, but hindsight is 20/20. There's a reason you made the decision you made at the time.*

It's important to fully believe that. If you're not clear about why you made the decisions you did, you can end up mired in regret, believing you made a mistake. Which is why this book, and the steps I've outlined for making decisions, are so important. As you work through each stage, clearly considering your options and motivations, the chance of regretting your decision is reduced substantially. And if you *do* end up regretting your decision, you will know beyond a doubt that you made the best decision at the time because you took the time to consider all the relevant issues.

The word *should* is a dangerous way of thinking. The best cure for regret is to look back and know, in your gut, that you were right at the time you made the decision. I think it's important to differentiate a no-regret decision that didn't work out the way you wanted versus a mistake.

I dislike the word *mistake* because it feels shame-y. But people use this word with me all the time. *I made a mistake.* In my practice, the people who specifically use the word *mistake* when reflecting on a big life choice are people who made decisions without following the Decision Crisis Playbook. Their decisions were likely made in panic mode and were all about short-term gain without thinking about the long-term impact. Or perhaps decisions were made that didn't honour their deciding values. So now their next normal isn't reflective of a life they truly wanted to live. Or they made decisions without pivot points or guardrails to keep them safe and happy in their next normal.

I would like to offer anyone who feels like they made a mistake the following: First off, it's okay if you made one. Making a decision when you're in panic mode is common. I think that's the reason I wanted to write this book. I've seen panic-mode decisions play out for long enough that I know they don't usually feel good after the short-term relief is over and often lead to regret. I realize, in the moment, it's hard to pull yourself out of panic mode and take on a growth mindset. But you *can* learn from bad decisions too and that's always hopeful.

Now that you know how to make no-regret decisions you don't have to worry: You know you have the power to change aspects of your life so they better reflect a world that makes you feel safe and happy.

If you hear yourself *should*-ing a lot, or using the words *mistake* or *bad decision*, you need to go back and revisit how you came to make your decision. Because, at the time, there *was* a reason.

## MEET JEFF

AGE: 64

RELATIONSHIP STATUS: Married

KIDS: 2 (ages 25 and 26)

"I try not to think about who we were before all of this," he said with a sigh. "It's almost painful."

I didn't say anything.

"That's the cruel thing about this disease." He rubbed his temples, eyes shut, clearly exhausted. "Sometimes I want to forget everything we were before, but I live for the 15 minutes of clarity I get each day. When she's my wife again."

I swallowed hard, trying to fight back my own tears.

Two years ago, at the age of 61, Jeff's wife, Amy, had been diagnosed with young-onset Alzheimer's. She was now 63, and her condition had deteriorated so rapidly, Jeff had no choice but to place her on a waiting list for a nursing home. A situation beyond his control had thrust him into an external decision crisis, and he had come in today to have me run some numbers.

"It's at least a year's wait for a private place, 2 years for anything subsidized," he said. "I should have put her on a list years ago. When things really started to get bad." He looked up at me. "I don't know if I can afford the support until she gets a spot or if I can even entertain the idea of a private residence." He shook his head. "What a mistake. I feel like such an idiot."

"You're not an idiot."

"No, I am," he said. "I kept delaying these decisions. Ignoring them. Like they would go away. Like somehow she'd just snap out of it, or someone would find a cure, or something. Now it's so late and I feel . . ." he trailed off.

"Feel what?" I pressed gently.

"Guilt, sadness, rage."

"I'm so sorry, Jeff."

"I barely recognize my life anymore."

"How so?" I asked.

"Well, her condition is getting so much worse. So much faster than I thought. We aren't sleeping. She's waking up every night panicking. I need more help. I can't believe I let it go on this long." His voice started cracking. "I failed her, you know?"

"You didn't. You haven't." I assured him.

"No. I have," he cut me off. "Again and again. I failed us both. I should have made different choices."

I heard the *should*.

He was staring at the table. "I'm in way over my head with this." He looked at me, his eyes brimming with tears. My heart broke for him. For Amy. For everybody.

"Jeff, there's no rule book for becoming a caregiver. There's no right or wrong. You don't learn this stuff in school. Everyone who becomes a caregiver is just doing the best they can and making the rules up as they go."

He rested his head on one hand.

"Sounds like you have a lot of regret," I said.

He nodded. "Which is why I don't trust myself to make decisions anymore. I'll screw them up."

"That's not true," I said.

"Well, I haven't handled this thing properly. I know that now and I'm stuck having to constantly make these insane choices."

"Regret is insidious," I said. "It makes us feel like we can't trust our gut."

"Exactly," he said. "And I feel myself getting bitter and angry."

"That's never fun."

"No, it isn't. There are these online people who have spouses with young-onset. I didn't join until recently even though practically everyone—my doctor, my friends, the neurologist, our kids—told me to get support from people going through what I was going through."

I nodded.

"But I didn't. So now, when I go on the forums, it's full of people who are just receiving the diagnosis of their spouse or someone close to them. And instead of wanting to help them, I'm—" He stopped himself.

"You're what?" I nudged gently.

"Well, I guess I'm jealous."

"What are you jealous of?"

"That they still have time to make those good decisions. It makes me furious."

He shook his head, almost in disbelief.

"That's not me." His eyes pleaded with me. "And I do help them, but I still feel so mad. It's so selfish. It's one of the main reasons I'm in therapy. I don't want to become bitter."

"Well, I think the fact that you're recognizing that is great. And you're still choosing to help others and you're getting help for yourself. You're doing all the right things."

I shifted in my chair a bit. "Can we try something a little different today?" I ventured.

"Sure?" he said.

"I'm putting on my life-coaching hat here," I smiled. "Where do you feel like you've failed?" I took out a piece of paper and a pen.

"What do you mean?"

"Well, you've said *should* a lot with respect to the decisions you've been making. I'm curious where all the *shouldas* are with your journey with Amy. The decisions you made that didn't work out the way you wanted. The ones you think were mistakes."

"Well, I *should* have sought advice from others in the same place as us when Amy first got her diagnosis. I *should* have put her on a list for a home much sooner. I *should* have saved more money when we were both working."

I wrote them down.

"Let's break these down, one by one. Let's start with *I should have saved more*. Why do you feel regret?" I asked.

"Amy got fired from her job because of her condition. Of course, we didn't know that she had Alzheimer's at the time, so her moods, forgetfulness, and lack of being able to plan things at work got her fired. So we have only had my income now for the last few years plus the added cost of support workers that I need. If we had saved more when we were younger, we would better be able to handle all these costs now and the potential cost of a long-term care facility. Maybe I'd even be able to keep the house once she's living there, but I know I'm going to have to sell to get the equity out."

"What were you able to do instead of saving?"

"You mean, what did we spend money on instead of saving it?" He grinned. The first true smile I had seen so far.

"Yes!" I said excitedly.

"Oh wow, travel. We travelled, built our house, put our kids through school."

"You're smiling. Ear to ear," I pointed out.

He nodded. "Those were good times."

"What was good about them?"

He shrugged. "They were normal. Happy. Family time. So carefree. We didn't think so at the time, but they were."

"Would you trade those memories for more money today?" I asked.

"No," he said, almost instantly.

"So what values do you think you were honouring by spending money back then on travel, your home, your kids?"

He thought about it. "*Hmm*. Family experiences, shared memories?" he asked. "Is that something?"

"Of course it is," I said. "And could you have reasonably predicted your current situation?"

"No. I mean every insurance salesperson tries to predict this, but no. What are the chances of young-onset? I mean, I'd be living an entire life of fear if I saw something like this coming and planned my whole life around it. We wouldn't have done anything."

"You know the saying *Everything happens for a reason*?" I asked.

"Sure."

"Do you think that choosing to spend money on family experiences, creating memories and stories rather than saving, happened for a reason?"

"Maybe."

I could tell he was thinking about it. "What would that lesson be?" I asked.

He thought about this–long and hard–then shrugged. "Maybe . . ." he said tentatively. "No."

"What?" I urged.

"I don't know, maybe the lesson there would be that Amy and I enjoyed life while we could and that's actually better?" It felt like he was asking my permission.

"Are you asking my permission to think that?" I asked.

His face went red. "I don't mean to. I just feel like it's . . . brazen to not regret saving more."

"Even if the fact that not saving more gave Amy and your family a wonderful, fear-free life?"

"Hearing it like that makes the shame feel misplaced, doesn't it?"

"Do you believe you made the best choice with respect to your money given the information and situation you had at the time?"

He paused. Then said, "Yes. I think I did."

I smiled and wrote it down. *Spent money creating family memories and stories.*

"Okay," I braced myself. "What about *Should have put her on a list earlier*?"

He shifted. I shifted.

"Why is this a regret?" I was internally cringing at my question. I wondered if I had crossed a line.

"If I had put her on a list earlier, it wouldn't be such a long wait now that her condition is so much worse. I'm looking at a 1- to 2-year wait, and I'm not sure I can emotionally, physically, mentally take care of her." Again, the emotion came flooding back to his voice.

"Why was it important for you to wait?" I asked gently.

His voice was cracking. "At the time, I wanted to honour

her wishes, and I thought that being home and in a familiar place with me would be best. I thought it would slow the decline, prolong her memories. I knew the wait was years-long for most people, but then I'd hear about someone getting a spot sooner, so I thought it would be okay."

I nodded.

His eyes welled. "I was also afraid to put her on a list. It freaked me out. She was so mentally with it at the time of her initial diagnosis. I didn't want her to be young and aware while she was in a long-term care facility. Does that make sense?"

I nodded again.

"She always said she never wanted to go to—" he broke down. He couldn't keep going.

"I'm so sorry, Jeff," I said, feeling helpless.

We sat there for some time.

He took a deep settling breath and cleared his throat. "Let's keep going."

"I'm curious about what values you think you were honouring by delaying putting her on a list?"

"Hers," he said, almost in a whisper.

I nodded.

"Was any part of this predictable?"

"Yes." He swallowed hard. "Alzheimer's is degenerative. There is no cure. I knew keeping her at home wasn't going to save her."

"So what was *unpredictable*?" I asked.

"How fast things deteriorated."

"How so?"

"I was always working with a 5-year timeline in my head. I don't know why."

"Go on."

"I knew she would keep getting worse, but I didn't expect it so soon. It's the reason why I didn't think I had to put her on a list right away. I felt like there was more time. But there wasn't."

"Could you have known how fast?"

He shook his head. "No."

"Do you think you'd do it differently if you could do it all again?"

He thought about this.

"Yes, but only a bit."

"What part would you change?"

"I always had this line in the sand. If she didn't know who I was, I'd put her on the list."

"A time guardrail," I said.

"Yes. Then it happened a few months ago for the first time. But I didn't listen to the voice in my head. I didn't act."

"Why not?" I asked.

"I don't know. Hope? Hope that maybe she'd plateau? Denial that she'd keep getting worse?"

"What was driving that?"

"My fear of putting her on a list and that she'd hate me. That even if it seemed like the disease had fully taken over her mind, that somewhere deep down she'd hate me for doing it." He shut his eyes.

"What changed your mind?"

"It's getting so bad. I'm not equipped to take care of her. Soon it's going to become unsafe for her and for me."

I nodded.

"Do you think you could have brought yourself to put her on a list before it got this bad?" I asked. "In all honesty."

He shook his head. "No. I think it had to get this bad so that I didn't have as much guilt."

"So what have you learned about this decision?"

"Well, that I've tried to honour Amy's wishes for as long as I possibly can."

I let that sentence hang in the air for a bit. It felt like an important realization.

"Knowing that, how does regret play into your decision now?" I asked carefully.

He gave a small laugh. "It doesn't. Or it shouldn't. Not when I think about it like this."

I wrote down *Honour Amy's wishes* and showed him the list:

- Spent money on family experiences, creating memories
- Honoured Amy's wishes

"These are the reasons you made the decisions you made at the time," I said.

He looked them over and silently nodded.

"How does it feel to see those?"

"Good. Relief actually."

"What's relieving about it?"

"Well, I guess I'm not as much of an idiot as I thought."

"Not at all," I said. "Knowing these were the driving forces behind your choices, do you believe you made the best decisions for your family at the time, even though things haven't worked out the way you planned?"

He thought about it and then nodded.

I smiled. "Me too."

We made a plan and strategy for his finances after that. We decided to borrow on a mortgage to pay for the extra costs of care and then downsize once Amy moved into a long-term care facility. We didn't know how long she'd be at home for—it could be a year, could be two. But at least he had a plan to support himself in the meantime.

I met with Jeff 14 months after our previous meeting. A lot had changed. Amy had moved into long-term care, he had sold their house, he'd paid off the debt he had taken on over the last year to pay for care support while Amy was still at home, and he'd downsized, moving to the city and into a rented apartment near Amy's long-term care home. These were big changes to his daily life that were never part of the plan.

Jeff had made an appointment to check in on his finances now that the dust had settled. He wanted to make sure that he had a plan in place to pay for Amy's care, make rent, and have enough money to survive retirement.

"That's a lot of change," I said.

He nodded. "Understatement." He looked tired but not as rough as the last time he was here. He had shaved and though the bags under his eyes were still there, they were less puffy.

"Are you sleeping more now?" I asked.

He shrugged. "Yes. Most nights. By the end there, Amy was waking up several times a night and was extremely agitated. She was so panicked. She didn't know who I was by then, so she'd scream at me to get out. Most nights, near the very end, I'd end up on the porch for a bit." He let out a long sigh. "I don't have that happening anymore now."

"I can't even imagine, Jeff," I offered helplessly.

"I hope you never have to."

I smiled. "So how can I help you today?"

He sat back. "I need a plan."

"New life, new plan," I said and I saw him recoil, cringing at my words.

"That feels like it did not resonate," I prodded.

"What?" he asked.

"I said *New life, new plan* and you reacted negatively." I pulled my shoulders up and scrunched my nose, imitating his body language. He looked down and realized his shoulders were up around his ears.

"Wow, I didn't even notice. Sorry." He gave his head a shake.

"Don't be sorry. I obviously stepped on some sort of emotional landmine."

"I guess so."

"What do you think made you so uncomfortable with me saying *New life, new plan*?"

He thought about it and ran a hand over the back of his neck.

"I guess the term *new life* bugs me."

"Why?"

"Because it implies permanency."

"Permanency to what?" I pressed lightly.

"To this life." He put his hands out while shrugging.

"What life?"

"This one. The one where I spent almost 3 years slowly watching my wife disappear. No matter what I did, or how I was there for her, she still forgot who I was. Sometimes it feels like it was all for nothing. Now we—or I—sold the house we built together. I live in an apartment, in a place I'd never wanted to live, so I can visit a woman who looks like my wife but isn't my wife."

I realized then, almost in disbelief, how much he'd been through.

"My kids say that I'm eroding," he added.

"What do you think they mean?"

"I think they think that I'm a shadow of my former self."

"How does that sit with you?"

"I don't think they are wrong," he admitted. "My therapist is helping me through the grief for the loss of my wife as I knew her and the trauma for the years I spent as her primary caregiver."

I nodded.

"It's helping for sure. To move through it," he added. "But I've been putting off this meeting with you since the move because of that whole *new life* thing."

"That's interesting," I said.

"I feel like if I make a financial plan with you, it's like admitting this is my life now. That it's not just *for now*. Or temporary."

"Well," I offered, "even temporary situations have plans."

"That's true. But I don't think my situation is temporary. This is my new normal," he said with a scowl.

"And you don't like it."

"Definitely not," he said. "This is not what I would have chosen."

"Given that life is unpredictable and no one knows what tomorrow will look like, let's not think of it as your new normal. Let's call it your next normal and realize that there may be more next normals in the future. Does that make sense?"

He nodded. "Yeah, and somehow *next normal* sounds less onerous."

"Good," I said, purposefully. "Now, can I offer a potentially controversial perspective here?"

"Sure?"

He finally smiled but I could tell he was nervous to hear what I was going to say.

"Obviously, you didn't choose for Amy to get Alzheimer's. That happened, and it's terrible."

He looked a bit defensive. I proceeded with caution.

"Once Amy was diagnosed, you had to make all kinds of hard decisions."

"Yes."

"We talked about many of them."

"Yes."

"And we worked through how each one of the decisions that you made honoured a very important core value."

He didn't say anything. But he also didn't tell me to stop, so I assumed I could keep going without making him shut down.

"So much of this next normal exists because of those very same choices."

"So you're saying the choices I made were because I wanted to live alone in an apartment without my wife after 3 years of caregiving?" He was getting more defensive and not less.

"Not at all," I said calmly. "Alzheimer's was not a choice. But the choices you made after the diagnosis were good choices, even if they led to a next normal that isn't what you planned before your crisis. Does that make sense?"

"I think so," he said, but I could tell he still had his back up.

"Becoming a caregiver for 3 years, selling the house you built together, ensuring the apartment you rent is near Amy's long-term care home . . . these were all extremely hard choices you made in service of your core values. Your core values of spending money on family experiences and creating memories and upholding Amy's wishes. Every single one of those choices was done in service of those values. There's nothing to regret."

"So does that mean I should like my next normal?" he asked.

"I'm saying you shouldn't regret the choices you made, even if you don't like where you are in your life right now."

"I agree that I wouldn't have done anything differently, but how do I get to a place where I actually want to make plans again?"

"Hope," I offered.

"Hope?"

"Hope for the future. That you believe that the crisis part of your life is over now, and you're in the next phase and you can start to build again."

He let out a long, slow breath. "Is the crisis really over?"

"That's for you to determine," I said.

He didn't say anything.

"But I do think your *decision* crisis is over."

"What do you mean?"

"Well, a decision crisis is often part of a personal crisis. But someone can have a decision crisis without being in a personal crisis. You had both. The decision crisis part of your journey is over. A decision crisis happens when there are very uncertain outcomes, very high emotional and financial stakes, and you have to make a series of difficult decisions at a really bad time in your life."

He nodded.

"So I'd argue that Amy's diagnosis of Alzheimer's is the event that began your personal crisis *and* your decision crisis. It was unexpected, had very uncertain outcomes, along with super-high emotional and financial stakes, and you had to make hard decisions every day at the worst time in your life. But those decisions have all been made. So at least we know that *that* part of your personal crisis is over. The decisions have all been made. The cards have fallen. You know where you stand now. There's no more uncertainty."

"Well, I mean, I don't know how long Amy will be alive for. I could live here for another 20 years or for 2. There *is* uncertainty, but the stakes aren't as high as before."

"How so?"

"All major questions have all been answered now, but the stakes at this point are more about my own personal well-being moving forward."

"Exactly."

"So maybe I have a decision crisis hangover," he said.

"What do you mean?" I asked.

"I'm definitely going to talk to my therapist about this. But I think I mean that I'm so used to being in a constant state of panic and intense decision-making on a daily basis, it's hard for me to come down. To believe it's, you know, over."

"What's over?"

"The decision crisis. And, I guess, my old life."

"Your caregiver old life or the time before?" I asked.

"Both, I think." He paused. "Selling the house was so painful. Necessary, of course, and I don't regret it, but it was painful."

"What was painful about it?"

"I made the choice alone. Amy never wanted to leave it. She used to joke that they'd carry her out in a pine box. So when I had to make that tough choice without her true consent or without her input, I felt guilty."

"Is the guilt the reason it was painful?"

"Yes. But also, I'm sad. We loved that house. We built the house *and* we built our family there. We've got roots. Deep ones. And I cut them off because I had to. I feel like the house was part of our family too. So it got lost in all of this as well."

I nodded. "It's almost like there needs to be a letting go of your past self. The part that expected to live in the house with Amy forever and also a need for you to bring the best parts of that past life forward into your new life."

"I'm not sure I understand."

"Living in the house when Amy was healthy was your old normal. Let's call that *house life*. Then, with her diagnosis, your life became *caregiver life,* and you needed to make all of these decisions. How it would all play out hung in the balance."

"Yes."

"And now we are here," I said. "In your *next* normal."

"Apartment life," he offered.

"Apartment life," I said. "I think you need to make peace with each one of these versions of your life."

"How do I do that?"

"Well, let's think. Let's start with *house life,*" I said. "What do you think you need in order to make peace with the fact that that version of your life is over?"

He thought about it for some time. "I keep looking at old photos. Photos I could barely look at over the last 3 years, while in caregiver life. It was too painful. But now I'm able to look at them nostalgically."

"What do you think that means?"

He smiled. "I think it means I'm enjoying my rose-coloured glasses."

"What do you mean by that?" I prodded.

"Well, I mean, we built the house and we loved it, but there were so many things about it that we wanted to change and never got around to. It was a never-ending renovation." He laughed. "It's funny how none of those things matter now. Like when someone passes away. Even if they were an ass-hole, everyone says nice things about them at the funeral."

"That's true," I said. Then it clicked. "What if you had, like, a funeral for your house life?"

He scrunched his face. "What?"

"Well, people have funerals to make peace with the fact that someone has passed away. To acknowledge that that person has passed on. Maybe going through old photos and fond memories of your house life is the same as someone going through photos and memories after someone passes away."

"I kinda like that idea," he said with a crooked smile.

"What do you like about it?"

"I like the idea of making peace with the fact that it's gone. Because I don't regret selling–it was just a painful choice. I think it would feel good to honour our time there in some way."

"That's new."

"I feel like the last 3 years there were so dark that much of the life we had there before was eclipsed somehow. I don't want the last 3 years to sour all the memories of that house. For myself and the kids."

"I hear you."

"So this idea of a funeral, where we can focus on the good memories from before Amy's diagnosis. Before caregiver life. It would be good for all of us, I think. But maybe not a funeral. Maybe like a celebration of life for the house."

I wrote down *Celebration of life for the house.*

"I love that," I said. "And what about the dark times? Caregiver life and the fact that that chapter is also over."

"It's funny. I'm obviously so happy it's over, but I feel lost a bit. When I was a caregiver, it was all encompassing. For better or worse, it gave me routine, structure, and purpose to my days. Now I find myself wandering around, not really knowing what to do with myself after work and on weekends if I'm not visiting Amy."

"What do you think you need in order to make peace with that time in your life?"

He smiled again. "What if we have a celebration of life for the house, but a totally inappropriate goodbye speech for the dark times."

"What do you mean?" I asked, smiling.

"I think I want to write a very honest goodbye speech about that time in my life. The kind that would make people squirm in their seats." He was grinning like a school kid.

I laughed out loud.

"No mourning. Just an 'I'm glad you're gone' type of letter," he said.

"Brutal honesty."

"Brutal honesty."

"I like it."

"Me too. I'm going to run it by my therapist as well. I think he will love it too."

I wrote down *Brutally honest goodbye speech to the dark times*.

"And what about your life today? Apartment life? What needs to happen for you to embrace your new journey there?"

He sat back in his chair. "I guess I just want to enjoy my day-to-day life. So much has changed. I don't have anything against living in the apartment. It's just that so much of my life has changed so quickly, and it's so different from anything I ever expected before. It doesn't feel like my life."

"It doesn't feel normal," I said.

"No," he confirmed.

"Well, sometimes when people are in panic mode, and their life has been turned upside down, I try to get them to 60% normal. It's a term I use to remind people that our normal is just a series of daily rituals and routines that we choose. The peace in that is that much of it can be replicated anywhere, anytime. I wonder if we can do that with you. To normalize your new life."

"That's an interesting thought," he said. "So how do I do that?"

"Well, what were some of your daily rituals of your life—your house life, before Amy's diagnosis—that brought you joy?"

He thought about it. "Oh, wow, I don't know. Is that weird?"

"Not at all," I assured him. "It's been a while and a lot has happened between that version of your life and today. Maybe walk me through a typical workday."

He looked up at the ceiling, trying to recall. "Well, we'd get up, walk the dog, read the paper. Go to work. Pretty basic."

"And after work?"

"We'd get home, Amy would usually cook—I'm a terrible cook—I'd take Mable, our dog, for a walk. Amy and I would talk about our day at dinner, maybe watch a show? God, it sounds so boring."

"Sounds like a lovely calm and peaceful life."

"It was. We were happy. We'd get out on weekends. Or host the kids when they were home from school."

I smiled.

"Where's Mable now? I didn't know you had a dog."

"Mable passed away. Just before Amy's diagnosis."

"I'm sorry," I said.

"Don't be. She lived a good life. In hindsight, that was a blessing. She was really old and on a lot of medication by the end. I don't know that I could have been caregiver to both of them at the same time."

"So which of these routines could you bring forward and recreate in your life today?"

"Well, I still go to work. And I've been thinking about getting a dog, actually. Someone to take care of and to keep me company. My therapist also thinks it's a great idea."

"I love it too."

"I think it will help to bring some of the normalcy back to my life too."

"What else?"

"It would force me to walk every day and be in nature. Other than that, I can't really talk to Amy about my day anymore."

"Why not?"

He looked at me. "Well, she's . . ." He smiled.

"Oh, I see."

"You visit her all the time, right?"

"Every day for now. I'm monitoring my feelings around that. Making sure that it feels like the right choice for her, for my mental health too. For now, it helps me feel normal."

"So an average workday, once you get the dog, will include some of the same routines and rituals as you did before becoming a caregiver," I said.

"I guess it will. I also think I need to keep visiting Amy with the kids on weekends. They are worried about me. I've been a bit of a shut-in since I moved."

"How do these routines uphold your core values of joy and family time and your goal to honour Amy's wishes?" I asked.

"Well, I think getting a dog would make Amy happy. She loved dogs. She would be happy I had a dog to keep me company. I also think that seeing the kids, going to work, walking the dog—all of those familiar routines—will help me feel normal."

"At least 60% normal," I said.

He smiled. "That's right."

I wrote it all down, and we made a plan for the financial part of his new life so that he was reassured that he was still in okay shape financially. We checked in by phone about a month later, after he got a dog.

I laughed. "Yay! I can hear a dog barking in the background."

"Melody, come here, girl," he said, and whistled.

"I like the name," I said.

"We lived on Melody Lane. That's where the house was."

I knew that already, but I was really happy to have him confirm that's why he named the dog Melody. "That's awesome. So how did everything go?"

"We're good."

I was happy to hear him say *we*. I knew it was him and the dog, but that meant he didn't feel alone in the same way anymore.

"What's good?" I asked.

"So the kids and I had a celebration of life for the house. It was so much fun and so important. Much more than I thought. For myself and for the boys."

"How so?"

"Well, we all picked our favourite memories in that house and we wrote them down, like a story. We got together and went to the road, sat on the curb, and read them out loud. I obviously checked in with the new owners. They were good with it."

I smiled.

"I cried like a baby," he said with a chuckle. "In front of the kids. And they cried. We all cried. For Amy. For the house. For all of it."

"That's really beautiful," I said.

"It was. And it was also the same day we picked up Melody. On purpose, of course. We picked her up afterward. It felt like the perfect way to say goodbye to the house and to start something new. I've felt lighter ever since."

"Fantastic," I said. "And what about the brutal goodbye speech to your dark times?"

"Ha!" he laughed. "I actually didn't do that."

"No?"

"No, it wasn't the right thing. I wanted to do it, but I realized that, for all the struggles and trauma, I'm actually grateful for that time in my life. To be Amy's caregiver. It was painful, scary, sad, and I was numb for much of it, but now that it's over and I look back on it, I'm proud of myself for making it through. For those moments where she was still Amy. For trying to honour her wishes as long as I could and for how it reprioritized my entire life."

I was in awe of him. "How did it reprioritize your life?"

"Some things that mattered before just don't matter now. Family, Melody, and our collective happiness matters. That's all I'm focused on. Workplace politics, or even money to some degree, don't even matter to me."

"I get that," I said.

"But I did do something else."

"Oh?"

"I ended up writing a brutal—I don't know—letter of complaint to Alzheimer's."

"To Alzheimer's?"

"Yes. To the disease. I wrote a nasty letter to Alzheimer's and told it exactly what I think of it and how I hate it." I could tell he was smiling.

"That's very original!"

"I never read it to anyone. I just wrote it. Five pages of rage, sorrow, anger, all focused on the disease. I politely asked it to go f*ck itself at the end." He laughed.

I laughed too.

"Yes, I was quite proud of myself for that one."

"Where is the letter now?" I asked.

"I printed it and left it with my important life insurance documents. Which means my kids will find it one day when I'm dead and will hopefully have a good laugh."

We laughed together, and then we both got quiet again.

"How is Amy?" I ventured.

He sighed. "About the same for now. But she's safe. And I take great comfort in the fact that she doesn't have panic attacks now at night and she seems calmer. I guess that's all we can hope for at this point."

"So how does your next normal feel?" I asked.

"It's starting to feel like regular normal. Not as new anymore. But I definitely feel lighter."

"That's good. You do sound like you've made peace with the fact that this is where you're at right now in your life."

"I have made peace," he said. "And I love that I can look back at everything that happened now without regret. The fact that I'm proud of it has brought me so much comfort. I didn't see it at first because my life was so dark for so long, but that time with Amy was important for us in ways that I am only starting to see now. I'm also glad I didn't hang on longer, until it was completely unsafe for everyone."

I didn't say anything. I just let us sit on the phone in silence for a moment.

"This isn't how I wanted my life to look at 65. But if Alzheimer's had to hit us the way it did, I'm glad I made the choices I did to end up where I'm at today. For better or worse."

"This is music to my ears," I said, and he laughed.

"Mine too, to be honest. In the thick of it, I really didn't know if I'd be able cope again. I still have a long way to go, but at this point I know I'll get there one day."

"You have hope again," I said.

"Hope. Yes," he replied.

• • •

After a decision crisis or a major life transition, your next normal may feel great. It might even feel like a total improvement. Or maybe it won't. It may feel strange, uneasy, and too different. It can also be hard to feel like your crisis is actually over until you're at peace with your new life. Coming to terms with the fact that your life has changed, that the decision crisis is over and that your new life has begun, is critical to being able to move forward, have hope, and make plans for the future again. If you can find peace, you can begin to embrace your new life even if it's not how you planned it.

## HOMEWORK: EMBRACE YOUR NEXT NORMAL

**Step 1:** Think back to a previous time in your life, before your decision crisis. List the daily rituals or routines that honoured your core values back then. Aim for 10.

**Step 2:** Brainstorm ways that you could bring some of these daily routines and rituals back into your life. This will ensure that you are actively cultivating a daily life that honours your core values.

**Step 3:** Create a goodbye ceremony for a previous time in your life that you are missing. How can you honour its memory and move on by saying goodbye?

**Step 4:** Create a goodbye ceremony for a previous time in your life that you resent. It may be a time in your life that was hard. While it's over now, it left an emotional scar. How can you acknowledge that time in your life and say goodbye?

# CHAPTER 12:

## Getting Ready for Next Time

When you're in a decision crisis, the stakes are high because your future, your next normal, is riding on your choices, and you want to like where you end up. In fact, you need to like it because your next normal eventually becomes your daily life, and we all want to like our daily life. The beauty of the Decision Crisis Playbook is that you can go back to the process every time life throws you a curve, as it inevitably will, knowing you'll make sound decisions that not only put you on a path forward but uphold your core values. Sometimes you'll find that you only need a few tools from the box to give yourself the confidence you need to choose a path forward.

If you don't believe you're good at handling a decision crisis because you regret how you've handled one in the past, using the Playbook will help you gain insight into *why* you made the choices you did and the reasons behind them. Once you've been through the steps, thought about your deciding values, perhaps identified where you intuitively made some guardrails or a micro timeline—or, more importantly, where you could have used those tools to set you on another path—you'll no longer think of those decisions as mistakes. Regret will fade because you'll have a better appreciation of who you were and what you were facing. An appreciation that allows you to be kinder to yourself, knowing you made the best choices you could with the tools and information you had in the moment.

It's important to come to terms with past decisions because, over time, living with regret, constantly beating yourself up over past decisions, erodes your confidence, making you doubt your ability to make the right choices. Eventually, that doubt bleeds into other areas of your life, robbing you of hope and creating prolonged anxiety about the future and resentment about the past. This toxic combination leaves you in a constant state of panic, unable to embrace your daily life because you're not at peace with the past and have no hope for the future. Using the Decision Crisis Playbook helps quiet that panic while building up your confidence. And that newfound confidence will carry you through any crisis.

## MEET LANAYA
AGE: 38
RELATIONSHIP STATUS: Single
CHILDREN: None

My client Lanaya is the perfect example of how holding on to regret about past decisions can impact your ability to make choices in the present. She was a corporate lawyer but never felt like that profession was a good fit and had struggled to find a career that worked for her.

She had made an appointment to determine whether or not she could afford to buy a condo or a townhouse, but when she started to talk, I realized her financial situation wasn't the issue. Her ability to trust herself was at stake because of a choice she had made years ago.

"My family encouraged me to go into law," she said. "And I went along because I didn't know what else I wanted to do. Turned out I was good at it, and I was offered a great-paying job in a firm specializing in corporate law right out of law school."

At the time, she was 26 and utterly miserable. As a lawyer, the money was great, but she admitted she felt like a "square peg in a round hole" and had become resentful of the work she was doing. She told me that every day she would wake up, look herself in the mirror, and give herself a pep talk before going into work. She had been at a crossroads decision crisis, where nothing unexpected had happened to her, no rug had been pulled out from underneath her, but her daily life didn't line up with her core values and doing nothing was no longer an option. She needed a change.

"I just quit one morning," she said. "For my partner, my boss, and my colleagues, it seemed out of the blue. Reckless. I even shocked myself."

"What was the final straw?" I asked.

She groaned. "I was working around the clock on a closing for 3 days. When the deal finally closed, I got home at 4 a.m. 4 a.m.! After averaging 3 hours of sleep for 2 nights, I just wanted to shower and sleep. Then I got an email invitation asking me to attend a critical meeting at 9:30 a.m."

"Whoa."

"After all my work for those 3 days, I thought I was going to get a break. If only to shower. I just lost it." She sighed. "It wasn't the first time something like that happened, and I knew it would not be the last. So I quit via email, had a shower, and went to sleep."

"How did that go?"

"I've spent a lot of time regretting that decision. Not the decision to quit—I'd been waffling on that for years—but *how* I did it still haunts me."

"Regret is tough."

"It is. I feel like it sort of poisoned my career."

"What do you mean by that?" I asked.

"Well, now I'm 38 years old and I still don't know what I'm going to be when I grow up." She laughed, but it was more than a little hollow. "I've tried on a lot of hats," she continued. "But every time I try to leave law to for another career, I inevitably end up going back." She rolled her eyes. "Anyway, how I quit that job has always been a massive regret. Whenever I go for job interviews, I'm still afraid that the person hiring me will find out that I quit by email all those years ago and think I'm unprofessional. I'm always worried that all my good work and effort will go unnoticed because it will be overshadowed by that massive drama."

"Regret has a way of robbing us of our confidence."

"Totally! I'm always apprehensive when trying to come back into law, so I end up going to smaller firms and settling for less money because I'm worried that the people I worked with back then are at the bigger firms now and that somehow I'll be seen as flighty or irresponsible. To make everything worse, my family has started pressuring me to 'grow up.' If I can't hold a job, I should at least buy something. A condo, a townhouse, any kind of property that will appreciate in value, set me up for retirement, etc., etc." She sighed. "Maybe they're right. Maybe I have been irresponsible for too long."

And there it was, the paralyzing self-doubt that comes from living with regret. That's when I realized that the initial focus of this meeting would not be her ability to carry a mortgage and all of the expenses that come with owning property. My first priority would be to help Lanaya find her way past the constant anxiety and self-doubt that kept her second-guessing her choices and to start rebuilding her confidence in her ability to make decisions.

Using the Decision Crisis Playbook to uncover the motivations behind those decisions—and seeing whether or not they aligned with her core and deciding values—was key to helping her move forward, stop second-guessing herself, and to restore her confidence in her ability to make decisions. Coming up with guardrails and mini timelines for any financial decisions about buying a property could come later. So I started up the whiteboard and let the Decision Crisis Playbook go to work.

I made two columns, one marked *Goals*, the other marked *Core and deciding values*, then I asked, "What do you think is happening in your life as a result of that lack of confidence?"

"I wind up settling for something I don't really want to do at a place where I don't really want to work, so I inevitably end up quitting again. It's a whole cycle." She raised her hands and let them fall. A gesture of defeat. "The problem is that I have a really varied skill set, and I'm interested in a lot of stuff, but nothing stands out as my *true skill* or top interest. So I end up defaulting back to law every time because the money is good. Yet I'm constantly panicking about what I'm going to do with my life."

I wrote *Eliminate panic* under *Goals* and then asked, "What's the panic about?"

"I feel like after so much waffling about what I want to do with my life, and all my poor decision-making, I'm having a bit of an identity crisis. Like, I don't know what I'm supposed to be doing for work. This professional life I'm living isn't me. I know there is something else for me, but I just don't know what that is."

I added *Solve identity crisis* to *Goals*. "What makes you think your decisions to leave and come back to law are poor decisions?"

"The way I quit the first time, was not, *um,* professional." She laughed in that same nervous, hollow way. "I haven't done anything like that since, but I can't help feeling like all these dramatic U-turns in my professional life make me flighty and flakey. My type-A personality is not impressed by the constant U-turns."

Like so many people, Lanaya's harshest critic was herself. I added *Avoid self-recrimination and judgment* to the list. "What's a U-turn for you?"

"A complete trajectory change," she said. "For example, the first time I quit law, I ended up working in a flower shop because I really love making flower arrangements and thought I would maybe one day open a flower shop."

"That doesn't sound like a bad decision," I said.

"I loved it, but it also wasn't for me. After working there for a bit, I realized that flower arrangements are something I love as a hobby, but it's not what I want to do 9 to 5. So I went back to law."

In the core values column, I typed *Flowers* in brackets. There was something there, we just needed to dig a little deeper for Lanaya to see it for herself. "What other U-turns have you taken?"

"I'm also a trained doula," she said. "And I worked at a real-estate staging place for a bit." She giggled a little then looked at the ceiling. "I think I've left and gone back to law like three or four times over the last 10 years."

*Doula* and *Real-estate staging* also went under core values, again in brackets. "Trying on different careers doesn't sound like bad decision-making. What makes you say that?"

"They're not just bad, they're disastrous if you think about my law career trajectory. The constant disruptions mean I haven't built toward becoming a partner. I've never created anything substantial in all my years in law and haven't stayed put long enough in any of my U-turns to build a career."

"So having measurable success is important to you?"

"You'd think so, yet all these years later, I still have no strong foundations anywhere. So, of course, my decisions to constantly try new fields only to revert back to law all feel like bad ones."

I typed *Measurable success?* and *Building strong foundations?* into the *Values* column and turned back to her. "Tell me what success and strong foundations mean to you."

"Something concrete that I could point to and say, *See? I did it. I'm officially a successful adult.*"

*Adulting?* went into the *Values* column. "Tell me about a time when you feel like you made a really good decision in your career."

"Well, looking back, I do think quitting that first corporate law job was a good decision." She smiled and shrugged a shoulder. "I just should've given 2 weeks' notice and not rage-quit."

"Do you think hindsight has given you the confidence to realize that it *was* a good decision?"

"*Hmm.* I never thought about it like that. I guess when I first quit, I didn't really know how everything would work out. I thought I'd never be able to work in law again. I thought I had just set my whole career on fire. But I have been able to return to law several times. Not to the position that I think I should be in or thought I should be in when I was in law school, but I guess I do know somewhere inside that I didn't blow up my entire career either."

I added *Try new things* to the *Goals* column. "What other decisions were good in your life?"

"*Hmm.* I don't actually know."

"Well, what are some things in your life that you're grateful for?" I asked.

"My apartment," she said without hesitation. "I rent this amazing three-bedroom apartment and it's so affordable because I've been there for 15 years. I've almost bought something a few times but never end up pulling the trigger on buying a house or a condo."

*Keep apartment* was also filed under *Goals*. "Why does that feel like a good decision?" I asked.

"Well, there's always been a lot of pressure to buy. From everyone. The media, my parents, even you probably think I should buy."

"I definitely have no real-estate agenda for you," I said with a smile.

"I know, but you know what I mean. The pressure to purchase real estate has always been intense and from everyone. Now that 40 is getting closer, it's worse than ever."

I nodded.

"I definitely have enough saved for a down payment, and when I'm working as a lawyer, I also have the cash flow to float a property on my own. Which is huge. But every time I look at real estate, everything always feels over-priced. And now that I think about it, my bigger worry is that, if I buy something, I'd have to keep working as a lawyer forever to support that choice."

"How so?"

"Unless I made partner, I'd have to maintain a certain income to pay my bills. I would be locked into the golden handcuffs of some law firm and could never leave to pursue something I really want to try if it paid less money."

"What has made you proud of the decision not to buy in the past?"

"Proud?" She thought about it. "I'm proud because renting affordably allows me to be flexible in my career."

Based on that pride, *Flexibility* went into the *Values* column, without a question mark.

"That's amazing. Can you give me some other examples of decisions you've made that you're really proud of?"

"I don't know. I guess being single?" she said.

*Single* made it into the list too. "Tell me about that."

"Like I said, I'm 38. I've been in many relationships. Good ones even, but never one where I felt like *This is it. This is the one,* you know? My last relationship recently ended because he was really pressuring me to have kids. He kept referring to my biological clock, trying to pin me down and make me into someone I'm not."

"That sounds tough."

"It is. I don't want kids. People don't get it. No matter how honest or blunt I am about it. It's like they think because I'm a woman, I must want to procreate. I've got nieces, and I love being an aunt. But I'm not going to change my mind on having children."

I added *No kids* and *Aligned partner* to *Values.* "Sounds like there are two decisions that you're proud of there. The decision not to be with someone who doesn't align with the life you want to lead and the decision not to have children."

"Yes," she said enthusiastically. "Absolutely."

"What makes you proud of those decisions?"

"I guess I'm very certain about not wanting children, and so I'm proud that I stuck to my guns."

"Can I check in on something with each of these big decisions that you're proud of?" I asked.

"Sure."

I turned the whiteboard around so she could see the lists. She leaned forward, studying it as I pointed to the *Core and deciding values* column. "We know that you can absolutely afford to buy a property, but you choose not to. If we look at *Flexibility, Being single,* and having the opportunity to try *Flower arranging,* being a *Doula,* and *Real-estate staging* as things that are important to you, that bring you true happiness, would you agree that we can put them all together under *Freedom* as a deciding value?"

She nodded. "Yes, absolutely."

"So what deciding value do you think you're upholding by choosing to rent instead of buying property?"

"Freedom," she said, almost instantly. She put her hands on her chest. "The idea of owning makes me freak out, unless I won the lottery."

I circled *Freedom* and moved on to *Aligned partner.* "And what value do you think is being upheld by deciding not to settle in relationships?"

"I think that I want a partner who loves all sides of me. I don't want to pretend."

"Authenticity?" I offered.

"Yes. Exactly." She snapped her finger. "Being my authentic self."

I put that on the board and circled it. "What about the decision not to have children?"

She mused on that for a bit. "I think both. Freedom and authenticity. I don't want to pretend I want to have kids—I love kids—I just don't want them personally."

I was smiling. "Let me get this straight. You set up your whole life to be authentic and free. To remain flexible in your career choices, love choices, and fertility choices. All of which shows amazing decision-making ability. Yet you resent the decisions you've made that actually allow you to live the life you want, to be free and authentic."

Now she was smiling too. "Wait, what?"

"Think about it." I turned back to the board. "It seems to me that *Measurable success* and *Building a solid foundation* have nothing to do with your own core values. I'd say those are values that other people try to impose on you. Does that sound right?"

She nodded emphatically. "It does. It really does."

I crossed them off the list and folded my hands on the desk. "You've made all these other decisions so that you can leave law at any time, be authentic to yourself, and remain free. But when you live authentically by trying on new career hats, for example, you regret it."

She looked me straight in the eyes, mouth opening, closing, opening, closing.

I laughed. "You didn't see the irony there?"

She laughed too, and this time it sounded genuine. "Not till now!"

"So can we reflect back on some of those career choices you think were a result of bad decision-making? How do they sit now that you've had this mini revelation?"

She laughed again. "Perfectly. I don't want a house and I certainly don't want to be a partner at a law firm! I want to try new things!

"So none of them were mistakes?"

"I guess not. It's just that I've been trained to think that being partner, owning property, are the be-all, end-all. The final goal. The arrival of adulthood. I'm an A-type achiever, so it's hard for me to not achieve the prescribed goal."

"But none of them are your goals, Lanaya. They never were. These are your real goals." I circled *New things* and *Keep the apartment* on the *Goals* list. "Law is strictly a means to an end. Something you use to support yourself financially while you try on different careers until you find one that fits. Returning to law now and then serves your goals of trying new things and holding on to your apartment, and you've more than achieved both."

She thought about this. "*Whoa!* You're right. I've never thought about that. I always feel like a failure because I'm failing at the law firm trajectory and there's never any certainty. My life is always changing."

"What's wrong with that?" I pressed.

"Nothing." She shook her head. "Nothing is wrong with that. I actually like it that way. But I feel like I'm not allowed to like it. I can't believe I've never seen it that way. That is what I want. I want my life to always be changing, and I've set up my whole life so that I could always have this ever-changing life, but then I punish myself for making the very choices that lead to an ever-changing life."

I smiled. "It seems to me that you've also achieved your goals of *Eliminating panic, Solving identity crisis,* and *Avoiding self-recrimination.*"

She laughed. "I have," she agreed. "And I feel such relief!"

"Relief from what?"

"Guilt?" she asked.

"And what's possible if you don't feel guilty about your past career U-turn decisions?"

Her eyes widened and a huge smile came across her face. "I feel excited!"

I laughed with her. "Good!"

"It means when I daydream about whatever random career choice I may want to explore next, or place I want to travel to, I don't have to shut it down or feel guilty or limited."

"You don't."

"I live a very affordable life. I don't have a lot of overhead. I've curated my life this way. I don't have to make partner or work at a top law firm to be successful. Law is there to provide me with a support system when I need it." She said this to herself. Almost affirming it.

"Sounds like adulting to me," I agreed.

"Yes!" she agreed, a wide grin on her face. "For me, success in my law career doesn't mean setting down roots and making partner. Success is the ability to come and go until I finally find what I'm looking for."

"I nodded, grinning with her.

"And I may never find what I'm looking for. And that's totally okay."

"Do you see that you're actually quite good at decision-making?"

She looked over at the list. "I guess I am."

"So how will this confidence in your decision-making impact you next time you want to leave law to U-turn your career?"

"Next time the itch comes, or I find myself in a place where I feel stuck, I think I can make decisions with less trepidation. Less questioning or waffling."

"With more confidence," I said.

"Yes. I'll trust myself next time I have to make a big decision."

"That's important."

"I guess it makes me feel ready for the next time pressure to buy or to settle down or to grow up comes at me."

"How does that preparedness feel?" I asked.

"Good. Very empowering, because life has a way of throwing curve balls and sometimes I create those curve balls for myself."

"For all of us, the stakes are always changing, but now you can trust that you know how to make good decisions, even in uncertain times. Decisions that you can be proud of. No-regret decisions."

"I like that. I won't be stuck second-guessing myself all the time."

"Exactly."

• • •

I'm not going to tell you how the story plays out. Want to know why? I still don't know and neither does Lanaya. She may be on this journey forever. But here's the power of the Decision Crisis Playbook: Rather than resenting her U-turn journey, or feeling guilty about choices that don't line up with the expectations of others, she's embracing it. Instead of seeing her inability to select a career and stay there forever as a constant identity crisis, she's embracing it as an adventure. Yes, she will have times of crisis, but she knows how to navigate them by making decisions she can be proud of later. She knows she's done it before and she can do it again. So can you.

## HOMEWORK: MAKE PEACE WITH A DECISION YOU FEEL WAS A MISTAKE

**Step 1:** Outline your *shoulds*. Use your own self-talk. What do you hear yourself saying to yourself about what you *should* have done differently? Write them out.

**Step 2:** Go through each *should* and write out why you made the decision at the time. What logic were you using? What gut instinct were you following? What did you think was going to happen at that time? What were you hoping for?

**Step 3:** What was important to you about the reasons in Step 2? What deciding values are reflected here?

**Step 4:** What benefits exist in your life from honouring the deciding values outlined in Step 3?

**Step 5:** What makes you proud of the reasons you cited in Step 3?

**Step 6:** What have you learned about yourself and what's important to you on this journey?

The point of this exercise is to accept that you can't go back in time. Only forward. But, hopefully, you can move forward without regret. If you feel like you've made mistakes, go back in time. Think about why you made that choice at the time. I bet you made those decisions for a reason. A reason that mattered back then. Your past self had no way of knowing how things would play out and, even if you had a hunch, you were probably honouring another deciding value by making the decision you did. You can learn from it. Mistakes make you ready for the next time.

# CHAPTER 13:

## You Got This

The Decision Crisis Playbook prepares you for any challenge life throws your way, giving you the confidence to embrace uncertainty in your life. You don't have to be afraid of what comes next because it's not really about the outcome. It's about how you make decisions today so you don't have regrets later on. The process gives you the ability to trust yourself to make no-regret decisions in the face of uncertainty—now, next year, or 10 years from now. It's comforting because we all know there will be a next time. That's life. It's a roller coaster. Full of ups and downs.

I still think back to those early days of the pandemic and the moment I decided I wouldn't move away, sell my business, and quit this book. That decision wasn't a quick fix, just as the email I sent to my agent telling her I was going to try to write the book wasn't the end of my decision crisis. In truth, it was the start. Once I was out of panic mode, I realized that quitting the book would have been a short-term, black-and-white trade-off, not a decision that would have truly honoured my long-term goals and values. But that doesn't mean things went smoothly from there. It was all so much messier than I could have imagined.

After I wrote that email, my best-case scenario would have been to write the book and hit the initial deadline. But with no childcare for 5 months and none of the regular supports in place, plus a business to navigate through an unprecedented situation, I simply couldn't. I had to pivot my timeline over and over again:

*I can't make this deadline.*

*I can't make this new deadline.*

*I'm so sorry, I need another extension.*

As an overachiever and Capricorn, failing to meet multiple deadlines was beyond difficult. But between the kids, the business, and trying to find a moment to breathe, I couldn't figure out a way to make it work. It was a full year of constantly trying to not give up. But sending that email refusing to throw in the towel had helped me find my way back to my own core values. I was determined to keep making decisions that Future Shannon would be proud of, which meant avoiding panic-mode decisions every day.

To accomplish that I started listening to good information from trusted people in my life—my family, my colleagues, my friends, and my publisher. That choice felt good in my gut because it aligned with my deciding values, reassuring me that, in the end, I wouldn't regret finishing this book.

Not only was writing this book one of the hardest things I've ever done professionally, it also represents a change in direction, bringing the world of life coaching into the world of finance. There's no knowing what that change will mean, but even now as I'm hurtling toward the finish line, each chapter represents my continuous decisions to keep going. Each page is my faith in the long game plan for my family, and each word is my decision to honour my deciding values over short-term relief from overwhelming fear. I see the page count and I'm so proud, I want to cry. I don't know how things will work out—that wheel is still spinning–I but I already know I don't regret it. No matter what happens from here, sticking it out was, and is, the better decision. A good decision. And I can't wait to see where my next normal is once this book comes out.

I have faith that all of the decisions I'm making today, tomorrow, and next month are the right ones for the long run. I'm comforted by the fact that I can trust my gut to continue to set up a life that I want to live in, regardless of how everything unfolds. I have hope and, most importantly, I have no regrets.

After reading this book, you know that a decision crisis doesn't give you time for slow, purposeful change. No matter what the situation, crisis demands you change your plans immediately, whether you're ready or not.

Looking back on the case studies, you'll see how the Decision Crisis Playbook can help get you over any hurdles life puts in your way and land you safely on the other side.

Through Susan's marriage crisis, you learned how to get to 60% normal to combat decision fatigue.

Shirley's circle of care showed you the importance of finding people in your same or similar circumstances—people you can talk to and learn from, making you feel heard and seen and less isolated in a turbulent time.

Clint's COVID condo crisis walked you through not only the importance of establishing micro timelines and micro goals but the steps you need to take to create your own, steps that help you gain short-term control during a crisis that's ongoing and unpredictable.

Calming Yasmin's worries after a divorce showed you how to use best- and worst-case scenarios to determine your deciding values and then prioritize them to guide your decision-making process.

Accepting that trying to control what life will look like 10 years from now is a fool's errand was a difficult lesson for Anika. Examining her options using short-term versus long-term predictability to reach decision predictability proved that there are ways to give yourself a feeling of control, if only in the moment, allowing you to make the best decisions possible in an impossible situation.

Finding out how Susan and Nicole created pivot points as well as time and money guardrails gives you tools to look ahead and identify moments in your own future when you may have to decide whether to carry on toward your goal or shift away from it. Establishing these guardrails ensures that you will recognize the moment when there are no more options.

Watching Anne and John struggle with their most difficult life decision highlighted what happens when you run up against your final time or money guardrail. Knowing there are no more options in advance helps take the emotion out of decision-making, letting you move forward without regret.

Kai's realization that tuning out the unhelpful voices and conflicting information in their life (and relying only on helpful voices and information) highlighted the importance of shutting out any sources that keep you in a constant state of anxiety. For Kai, that meant muting most social media, all news feeds, and those individual voices that robbed them of their peace of mind. Silencing those voices in your own life allows you time to breathe and think, and then make the best decisions for yourself.

Seeing how Jeff came to terms with his next normal after his wife was diagnosed with Alzheimer's offered reassurance that even in your darkest moments there is a way forward. Like Jeff, your next normal will probably be a blend of good and bad that looks nothing like the life you had imagined. But that doesn't mean it won't be a good life filled with future possibilities and, more importantly, hope.

Lanaya's struggle with regret over past decisions let you see that not every situation requires the use of every step in the Decision Crisis Playbook. By focusing on the deciding values tools, Lanaya discovered that her deciding values were very different from the ones others had imposed upon her all of her life. Choosing the tools you need to get you through your own crisis allows you to make no-regret decisions that will still make you proud years from now.

That pride, that confidence in your decisions, is what helps you fully embrace your next normal, because you aren't constantly comparing your present situations to your past in a negative way. This happens when you have a daily life that reflects your main core values, your deciding values. Embracing your next normal may not happen right away. It often takes time before you're able to see your choices more clearly. But if you make good decisions, you'll cultivate a new daily life that reflects your values and fills you with confidence for the future.

Following the Decision Crisis Playbook will aid in your decision-making so you'll arrive on the other side of your crisis sooner. But it will also help you to make confident decisions that will help you to embrace your next normal so you don't end up in a permanent state of regret, which will only lead you into a never-ending cycle of crisis.

I don't think it's possible for anyone to avert or avoid a personal crisis in their life. At some point, an unexpected situation will throw you off course and require you to make difficult decisions. Or you'll reach a crossroads where something in your life has to change and doing nothing is no longer an option. Hard decisions must be made. No matter which type of crisis you may find yourself in, you'll need to decide your way through the crisis in order to reach your new life safely. Your next normal.

If you're in a decision crisis right now, you're already actively building your next normal. It's kind of fun to think of it that way because *you* get to decide what your next normal looks like and how you embrace it, knowing you made the best decisions possible, given the circumstances.

After reading this book, you now know:

1. How to get yourself out of panic mode so you can make decisions in a growth-oriented mindset (even if only for a moment).
2. How to create a circle of care to help you feel heard and seen and less isolated.
3. How to figure out your deciding values so you make choices that reflect your core values, which will lead to happiness in your next normal.
4. How to look for and assign short-term predictability to give yourself some decision predictability and control what you can.
5. How to stay safe and avoid regret by setting pivot points and time/money guardrails.
6. How to embrace your next normal, even if it didn't work out the way you hoped.

Once you understand how to make no-regret decisions, you will make them for the rest of your life. The formula is proven and, best of all, it's repeatable for any situation. You can trust your decisions today, tomorrow, forever, no matter what life throws at you.

You got this.

*xo*
Shannon

# ACKNOWLEDGEMENTS

Most of this book was written during COVID-19 lock-downs with no childcare, a baby, and a toddler. It was one of the most anxious and chaotic times of my life. I did not think I would make it to the finish line and tried to quit many times. That's why I am so proud of this book. To have pushed through and just keep writing was, truly, a series of no-regret decisions.

This book would not have been written without the love, support, and patience of so many. Thank you all so much.

Mom—Thank you for being my number-one fan and for helping me continue to find my way to a no-regret decision with this book. I love you.

Matt–Thank you for being the ultimate partner, co-parent, work-from-home colleague, and best friend during this roller coaster. I love you and couldn't have done it without your endless support (taking on most 4:45 a.m. toddler morning shifts and your delicious coffee-making skills). You got me and I got you.

My family and friends–Thank you for cheering me on over teary virtual hangs and helping me make it to the finish line.

My editor, Janice Zawerbny–Thank you for your patience and continuous support. We made it! You always knew we would, even when I was filled with doubt.

My agent, Martha Webb–For believing in me and this book from the get-go and for supporting me no matter where I was at during this chaotic journey.

My publisher, HarperCollins Canada–You are all so wonderful. Thank you for your endless patience and vision for this book.